# Nihongo Notes

# 日本語ノート

Language and Communication
ことばとコミュニケーション

Vol. 2

Osamu Mizutani & Nobuko Mizutani

水谷 修・水谷 信子

The Japan Times

First edition: February 2011

English proofreading: Janet Ashby and Jon McGovern
Layout design: Asahi Media International Inc.
Jacket design: Akio Udagawa
Printing: Nikkei Printing Inc.

Published by The Japan Times, Ltd.
5-4, Shibaura 4-chome, Minato-ku, Tokyo 108-0023, Japan
Phone: 03-3453-2013
http://bookclub.japantimes.co.jp/

ISBN978-4-7890-1425-0

Printed in Japan

# PREFACE

In the preface to the first volume we related how the first "Nihongo Notes" column was published and was followed by 349 more. We will not repeat that story here, but want to add that "Nihongo Notes" has been translated into other languages. The first 70 essays were translated from English into French by Marie-France Delmont Hosaka and Renée Lagache Horiuchi, and into Spanish by Virginia Meza and Luis A. Davalos. We heard that some pieces were translated into Chinese and Korean, but we never received any official notification of that. All 350 columns were translated into Thai by Dr. Preeya Ingkaphirom, who recently sent us her work. And we finally translated all 350 of them into Japanese in 1988-89—the Japanese texts which are used in this edition.

In this new edition, 50 out of the 350 columns are included in volume one, and another 50 in volume two; they are in both English and Japanese. Of the two volumes, the first mainly includes pieces discussing the social and cultural significance seen in daily greetings and common expressions. The second volume focuses on the subtle meaning of common phrases and expressions of politeness. In all of them we discussed the ways of thinking of the Japanese people in human relationships and societal life, rather than merely explaining the verbal meaning of phrases.

The original aim of "Nihongo Notes" was to arouse interest and deepen understanding in Japanese among the readers; we tried to present our discussion with a touch of humor and of the unexpected for easy reading. For example, *"Kaette-kudasai"* (Please go home) introduces the misunderstanding and laughter caused by a literal translation of an English phrase. And we added that the word *kaeru* (come back) reflects people's attitude toward their hometown or workplace. Also, we avoided using technical terms in explanations; when explaining the use of *ta,* which refers to past action, in the expression *"yaseta hito"* (thin person), we cautioned the reader not to say *"yaseru hito"* since it would mean someone who loses weight rapidly in front of your eyes, instead of relying on grammatical terms.

Understanding the Japanese language should be understanding how it is used in Japanese society. For a more profound understanding of the Japanese language and society, it is essential to understand what is in the speaker's mind when using an expression, rather than to merely scrutinize the verbal meaning or to make a word-to-word comparison with other languages. The authors sincerely hope that the discussions in this book can help the reader achieve such an understanding.

We heartily thank the editors of The Japan Times for planning and working hard on this edition of *Nihongo Notes.* Finally, we want to express our gratitude to Ms. Janet Ashby for correcting the English in most of the articles and giving us invaluable advice.

January 2011
Osamu and Nobuko Mizutani

par osamu mizutani
nobuko mizutani

The **Japan Times**, Ltd.

---

### *Doomo*
### どうも
### (Vraiment)

Un mot tourmente M. Lestude en ce moment. C'est *Doomo*. Les dictionnaires japonais-français le traduisent par "vraiment" ou "d'une manière ou d'une autre" mais il a l'impression que son usage réel s'étend bien au-delà.

Ses collègues de bureau, par exemple, emploient *doomo* dans beaucoup d'autres cas. Ils disent *Kinoo-wa, doomo* (Hier, vraiment) quand ils se rencontrent. Ils disent simplement *Doomo* pour remercier et s'excuser, et déclarent encore *Ja doomo* quand ils se quittent.

*Doomo* s'emploie aussi pour abréger une réponse. Quand M. Lestude a demandé à M. Takada où en étaient ses études d'anglais, celui-ci a répondu *Doomo-nee*. Il ne voulait pas dire qu'il avait fait de grands progrès. C'était précisément le contraire.

La plupart des Japonais, probablement, ne mesurent pas combien ils usent ou abusent de ce mot. Littéralement *Doomo* signifie "de toute façon" ou "peu importe mon point de vue". En réalité, on l'utilise avec des sens variés. Deux emplois de *Doomo* sont particulièrement fréquents: l'un comme formule des relations sociales, l'autre comme indication d'un point de vue négatif.

Dans les relations sociales, il est employé seul et signifie "merci", "pardon", "excusez-moi", "merci d'être venu", "désolé de vous faire perdre votre temps", pour ne donner que quelques exemples. Les deux derniers sont l'équivalent de "salut" et d'"au revoir". Dans ces expressions, ce qui suit

22

*doomo* est omis. Par exemple dans le cas de *doomo arigatoo-gozaimasu*, *arigatoo-gozaimasu* est sous-entendu.

Le deuxième emploi est aussi très courant. Si vous posez une question à quelqu'un et qu'il vous répond juste *watashi-wa doomo . . .* (*litt. Moi, de toute façon*) d'un ton hésitant, il veut dire qu'il ne sait pas quoi répondre. Ou bien encore, si vous demandez l'opinion de quelqu'un sur quelque sujet et que la réponse est *Doomo* ou *Doomo-nee*, cela signifie que celui-ci n'est pas d'accord. C'est ainsi que M. Takada a utilisé *Doomo* quand M. Lestude l'interrogeait sur ses études d'anglais.

*Doomo* change de sens non seulement selon la situation mais aussi selon le ton dont on le dit. Si vous le prononcez rapidement, cela semble désinvolte. (Certains disent rapidement *Doomo, doomo* en accueillant les gens; ceci paraît très familier et ne convient pas quand vous voulez être respectueux ou courtois.) Mais si vous le prononcez lentement, cela semble sincère et poli. Pour exprimer un désaccord, il se dit d'un ton hésitant, comme en suspens.

23

*"Doomo"* (Vraiment)

# はしがき

　英字新聞 The Japan Times の週1回の column に "Nihongo Notes" が初めて掲載され、年月とともに回を重ねて350編となり、うち100編が今回新しく出版されることになった経緯については第1巻の序で紹介したので、ここでは繰り返さない。ただ、ひとつ付け加えておきたいことは、この記事は最初は英語で書かれたが、のちいくつかの翻訳版が出たことである。最初は"Nihongo Notes 1"の70編がフランス語（Marie-France Delmont Hosaka ／ Renee Lagache Horiuchi 訳）とスペイン語（Virginig Meza ／ Luis A. Davalos 訳）に訳された。中国語版と韓国語版もあると聞いているが、著者は知らされていない。タイ語版はプリヤー・インカピロム博士によって volume1〜5まで訳され、最近その寄贈を受けた。"Nihongo Notes 5" が出たあと、日本語版を望む声があって、著者自身が1988年6月〜89年12月に和訳した。それが今回の対訳版の和文である。

　今回の再版ではこれまでに出た "Nihongo Notes 1〜5" 350編から第1巻として50、第2巻として50の計100編が日英対訳の形で出版される。うち、第1巻は「文化」編として日常生活で使われる挨拶や表現にひそむ社会的・文化的な意義を中心とし、第2巻は語句の陰影と待遇表現などを主としている。いずれも単なる語句の詮索を超えて、日本語の表現にみる対人関係意識を検討するもの、日常の挨拶などについての社会言語学的な解釈を論じるものである。

　本来の目的が一般の読者の理解と興味を促すものであるから、楽しく読めるように意外性とユーモアを含むものとした。第2巻の「帰ってください」は、英語話者が英語の "come back" の影響で「また来てください」と言うべき時に「帰ッテクダサイ」と言ってしまったという実例をあげ、誤解と笑いが生じたことを扱っているが、それだけでなく、使用実態として「帰る」が自宅のほかに故郷や職

場にも使われる場合をあげて、社会生活と意識の変化にも光をあてた。また、文法的な解説にも専門的な術語の使用は避けた。「うちへ帰った時ビールを飲む習慣がある」のような「た」の使用について述べた記事「やせる人」では、「アスペクト」のような術語を用いず、「やせる人」と言うと目の前でだんだんやせていく人のようでおかしいから「やせた人」と言う、という印象的でユーモラスな説明をした。

　日本語を理解することは日本語を使っている社会を理解することである。日本語と日本人社会に対する理解を深め、その理解を今後の国際社会に生きる上で役立てるためには、単なる語句の詮索や、語句単位での外国語との比較を超えて、日本語を使う人の心に思いを致すことが大切である。そのためにこの書を参考にしていただければ、著者としてはまことに幸いである。

　この書を企画し、労をいとわず力を尽くしてくださった The Japan Times 社の編集者にお礼を申しあげる。最後になったが、350編の大部分について英文の修正と助言にあたってくださった Janet Ashby さんに深い感謝の意を表したい。

2011年1月　水谷修・水谷信子

# Index　もくじ

## Chapter 2: Difference from English
### 英語との違い

## Chapter 3: Human Relationship
### 人と人との関係

●本書は『Nihongo Notes 1～5』(ジャパンタイムズ刊) および、その日本語訳版である『外国人の疑問に答える日本語ノート 1～4』(同) から「ことばとコミュニケーション」に関する50編を選び、再編集したものです。

# Chapter 1

# Situational Phrases

場面に応じたことばづかい

In this chapter we offer help to foreign learners of Japanese who want to speak in a more appropriate and sophisticated way. At the same time we hope we offered assistance to those trying to answer foreigners' questions about Japanese.

How does *30-pun-shika arimasen* differ from *30-pun dake arimasu*; how does *Atsuku natta-n-desu-ne* differ from *Atsuku narimashita-ne*; how does *Okutte-kimashita* differ from *Okuri-mashita*; how does *Kowashite-arimasu* differ from *Koware-mashita*? Does *Ichido ome-ni kakaritai-to omoimasu* mean that the speaker wants to see someone just once and no more?; they seem very short and simple but play an important role in communication.

Also, is *Takada-san-tachi* the same as Mr. and Mrs. Takada? Does saying *Ocha-demo nomimasen-ka* imply drinking something other than tea? What does *Tekitoo-ni yatte-kudasai* mean? What does *mo* in *Sen-en-mo daseba* mean? We tried to answer such questions bothering serious students of Japanese.

この章では、特に外国語として日本語を学習した人が、さらに適切で豊かな表現が使いこなせるようにという観点から、語法的に疑問のある点を解説し、理解を促進することを目的としている。また同時に、学習者の疑問に答えようとする日本人の助けにもなると考えられる。

　「30分しかありませんから……」は「30分だけある」とどう違うか、「暑くなったんですね」は「暑くなりましたね」とどう違うか、「送ってきました」は「送りました」とどう違うか、「こわしてあります」は「こわれました」とどう違うか、「一度お目にかかりたいと思います」は一度だけ会いたいのか、というような、語法的な疑問に答えるものである。

　また、「高田さんたち」は「高田さん夫婦」か、「～たち」はどう使われるのか、「お茶でも飲みませんか」の場合はお茶のほかの何か飲むのか、「適当にやってください」の「適当に」はどんな意味か、「千円も出せば……」の「も」は何を表すのか、というような語句について、真剣に日本語を学ぼうとする人の疑問に答えようとした。

# 'Hai'-to 'Iie'
## 「はい」と「いいえ」
### 'Yes' and 'No'

During the tea time yesterday afternoon Miss Yoshida placed a bowl of chocolates on the table and left the room for the tea pot. When she returned and looked at the bowl, she seemed to be wondering about something. Then she turned to Mr. Takada and said half-jokingly

*Takada-san, kore, tabemasen-deshita-ka.*
(Didn't you eat some of this, Mr. Takada?)

Mr. Takada looked surprised and answered quickly

*Iie, tabemasen-deshita-yo.*
(No, I didn't eat any.)

Mr. Lerner thought that *Ee* should have been used in place of *Iie*. He had learned that Japanese answer negative questions differently from English-speaking people. Namely, while English-speaking people say "No" when agreeing to a negative question as in

A: Didn't you go with him?
B: No, I didn't.

Japanese say *Ee* or *Hai* (more polite) as in

A: *Issho-ni ikimasen-deshita-ka.*
B: *Ee* (or *Hai*), *ikimasen-deshita.* (lit., Yes, I didn't go.)

# 「はい」と「いいえ」

## 'Yes' and 'No'

　昨日の午後のお茶の時間に、Miss Yoshida はチョコレートの入った菓子皿をテーブルの上に置いて、ポットを取りに出て行った。帰ってきて菓子皿を見ると、何か不審に思ったらしく、Mr. Takada のほうを向いて、冗談めかして、

　　高田さん、これ、食べませんでしたか

とたずねた。Mr. Takada はびっくりした顔をして、急いで、

　　いいえ、食べませんでしたよ

と答えた。

　この場合は「いいえ」でなく「ええ」と言うべきではなかったのか、と Mr. Lerner は思った。日本語では、否定形の疑問文に対して英語と違う答えかたをする、と習ったことがある。つまり、次のような場合、英語では、

　　A：Didn't you go with him?
　　B：No, I didn't.

と "No" で答えるが、日本人は「ええ」や「はい」（「ええ」より丁寧）で、

　　A：一緒に行きませんでしたか
　　B：ええ（はい）、行きませんでした

と答える。だから Mr. Takada も、Miss Yoshida の質問に同意していたのだから、

15

Therefore Mr. Takada should have said

*Ee, tabemasen-deshita.*

because he was agreeing with Miss Yoshida's question.

*      *      *

It is true that the listener answers *Hai* or *Ee* if he agrees with the speaker regardless of whether what follows is in the negative or affirmative. But the most important question is what is meant by "agree." In social communication the listener answers *Hai* when he is going to comply with the speaker's expectation or intent, rather than with a fact the speaker has referred to. Therefore it is possible that either *Hai (Ee)* or *Iie* can be used to answer the same question, depending on the situation.

If Miss Yoshida had asked *Kore, tabemasen-deshita-ka* simply to make sure that Mr. Takada hadn't eaten some of the chocolates, he would have answered *Ee* to show his agreement. But actually she sounded as if she suspected that Mr. Takada had eaten the chocolates before he was asked to, and the question implied criticism. Consequently Mr. Takada said *Iie* to show his denial of her suspicion.

There are exceptions to this use of *hai* and *iie* and some, mostly young, people use *hai* and *iie* more like English-speaking people. But fundamentally the use of "yes" and "no" in Japanese is determined by the relationship between the speaker and the listener, rather than by sheer facts.

(September 30, 1979)

　　ええ、食べませんでした

と言うべきだったのではなかろうか……。

＊　　　　　＊　　　　　＊

　質問の形が肯定形でも否定形でも、相手に同意する時は「はい」「ええ」と答える、ということは事実である。しかし、最も重大な問題は、「同意」の意味である。社会的なコミュニケーションの場では、事実に同意する場合よりも、相手の期待や意図にそおうとする時に、「はい」と答える。したがって、同じ質問でも、状況によって「はい（ええ）」と「いいえ」の使い分けが違ってくるのである。

　Miss Yoshida が Mr. Takada に「これ、食べませんでしたか」ときいたのが、単にチョコレートを食べたかどうかを知るためであったら、賛意を示すために「ええ」という答えが出たであろう。しかし実際には、彼女の口調が、すすめられもしないうちからチョコレートを食べてしまったのだと、疑ってかかっている調子で、質問が批判を含んでいた。それで Mr. Takada はその疑いを否定するために「いいえ」と言ったのである。

　この「はい」と「いいえ」の用法には例外もある。主として若い人たちであるが、「はい」「いいえ」を英語的に用いる人がいる。しかし、日本語の「はい」「いいえ」は基本的には、事実そのものよりは話し手と相手との関係で決まるものである。

（1979.9.30）

# *Kore-ga ii-desu*
## これが いいです
### I want this one

Mr. Lerner wanted to buy a tiepin for himself at a department store. The salesgirl started placing several pins one after another on the counter in front of him. He liked the first one she showed him, so he said

*Kore-wa ii-desu.*

meaning "I want this one (lit., This is good)," but the girl quickly moved it aside and put another one in its place, so he pointed to it and said that he wanted it. Then the girl said

*Aa, kore-ga ii-n-desu-ka.*

(Oh, you mean you want this? —lit., Oh, is it that this one is good?)

as if she was surprised. Mr. Lerner wondered if the difference between *ga* and *wa* can make that much difference.

*　　　*　　　*

Yes, a single particle can change the meaning of a statement completely. To indicate what or which one is good, one says

*Kore-ga ii-desu.*

or *Kotchi-ga ii-desu.* Similarly, to a question about which one you would like, you should say

# これがいいです

## *I want this one*

Mr. Lerner はデパートで自分のネクタイピンを買おうと思った。店員がカウンターの上にいくつかのピンを次々に並べ始めたが、その最初のピンが気に入ったので、

　　　コレハイイデス

と言った。「これがほしい」のつもりであったが、女店員はさっさとそれをどけて、別のピンをそこにおいた。Mr. Lerner が最初のピンを指さしてそれがほしいのだと言うと、

　　　ああ、これがいいんですか

と驚いたように言った。「は」と「が」の違いがこんなにも重大な結果を生むものかと Mr. Lerner は思った……。

　　　　　　　*　　　　　　*　　　　　　*

　その通り。わずかひとつの助詞の違いでも意味が全く違ってしまうことがある。何がいいか、どちらがいいかを示すには、

　　　これがいいです

あるいは「こっちがいいです」と言う。同様にどれがほしいかときかれて答える時は、

*Kore-ga* (or *Kotchi-ga*) *hoshii-desu.*

Or, if someone asks several people which one of them is Mr. Kato, Mr. Kato will say

*Watashi-ga Katoo-desu.*

On the other hand, *wa* is used in a situation where you are asked who or how someone or something is. Mr. Kato will say *Watashi-wa Katoo-desu* when he is asked who he is; *Watashi-wa genki-desu* is used when you are asked how you are. But the phrase *watashi-wa* is not said when it is understood. Thus to the question "How are you?" one usually says *Genki-desu* instead of *Watashi-wa genki-desu.* And to introduce oneself, one usually says *Katoo-desu* rather than *Watashi-wa Katoo-desu.*

In the case of Mr. Lerner buying a tiepin mentioned above, he should have said *Kore-ga ii-desu* to mean that he wanted it. *Kore-wa ii-desu* can mean that you don't want it, depending on how it is said. If you pronounce *ii-desu* strongly as

*Kore-wa II-DESU.*

it means "No, thank you." Mr. Lerner could have succeeded in conveying his desire if he had emphasized *Kore* as

*KORE-wa ii-desu.*

Or, if he had added *nee* as

*Kore-wa ii-desu-nee!*

(January 20, 1980)

　　これが（こっちが）ほしいです

と言う。また、何人かの人の集まっているところへだれかが来て、どの人が加藤さんかとたずねたなら、Mr. Kato は、

　　わたしが加藤です

と答えるであろう。

　一方、「は」のほうは、ある人がだれであるか、あるものがどうであるかを問われた時に用いる。Mr. Kato も、「どなたですか」ときかれたら、「わたしは加藤です」と言うであろう。「元気ですか」ときかれたら、「わたしは元気です」と言う。しかし、「わたしは」の句は、自明の場合には言わない。したがって、「いかがですか」ときかれたら、「わたしは元気です」と言うより「元気です」と答えるほうが普通である。また自己紹介をする時も、「わたしは加藤です」より、「加藤です」のほうが普通である。

　Mr. Lerner がタイピンを買った上記の場面では、自分の意志を伝えるためには「これがいいです」と言うべきであった。「これはいいです」は言いかたによっては、「ほしくない」の意味になる。「いいです」を強くして、

　　これはいいです

と言ったら、「いりません」の意味になる。逆に「これ」を強調して、

　　これはいいです

と言うか、あるいは「ねえ」を加えて、

　　これはいいですねえ！

と言っていたら、Mr. Lerner はほしいものを手に入れるのに成功していたかもしれない。

（1980.1.20）

# *Sanjippun-shika arimasen-kara*
## 30分しか ありませんから…
*I only have 30 minutes, so. . .*

A few days ago Miss Yoshida asked Mr. Lerner if he could help her with something that day. Mr. Lerner was rather busy and could spare only 30 minutes to help her. Since he did not like to hurry with work, he said

*Kyoo-wa sanjippun-dake arimasu-kara . . .*

meaning "I only have 30 minutes today, so . . ." He expected Miss Yoshida to understand that he didn't have time to do it, but she again asked *Ja, yatte-kudasaru-n-desu-ne.* (Then you'll do it for me, won't you?) When Mr. Lerner said that he was busy that day and would rather do it the next day, Miss Yoshida left, looking a little confused.

Mr. Takada said later that Mr. Lerner should have said

*Kyoo-wa sanjippun-shika arimasen-kara . . .*

to mean that he only had 30 minutes so he couldn't do it.

*       *       *

Mr. Lerner had learned the expression ". . . *shika* plus the negative" which means "only . . . ," but he thought that it meant the same thing as ". . . *dake* plus the affirmative" and had never used it very much.

The two expressions are not equivalent; . . . *dake* is used to indicate the exact amount, meaning "neither more nor less than . . . ," while . . . *shika*

# 30分しかありませんから…

## I only have 30 minutes, so. . .

　数日前 Miss Yoshida が、きょうちょっと手伝ってくれるかと、Mr. Lerner に
たずねた。その日はいそがしくて、30分しか彼女のために割くことができなか
った。急いで片づけるのは好まなかったので、

　　　キョウハ30分ダケアリマスカラ……

と言った。時間がなくてできないということがわかってもらえると思ったのだ
が、Miss Yoshida は重ねて「じゃ、やってくださるんですね」と言う。きょうは
いそがしいからあしたにしたいと言うと、キツネにつままれたような顔をして行
ってしまった。

　あとで Mr. Takada に聞くと、それなら、

　　　きょうは30分しかありませんから……

と言うべきだったのだそうである……。

　　　　　　　　　　＊　　　　　　　＊　　　　　　　＊

　Mr. Lerner は "only . . ." の意味で「しか＋否定形」を習ったが、「だけ＋肯定
形」と同じだと思ったので、あまり使わなかった。

　この2つの形は同価ではない。「〜だけ」は正確な数量を表し、「〜より多くも
少なくもない」という意味を示すが、「〜しか〜ない」は、その数量が極めて少
ないか少なすぎるの意味である。したがってだれかが「30分しかありませんか

... *nai* means that the amount referred to is very small or too small. Therefore if someone says *Sanjippun-shika arimasen-kara* the listener immediately understands that the time is so limited that the proposal cannot be accepted. On the other hand, if someone says *Sanjippun-dake arimasu-kara* it means that the speaker has exactly 30 minutes without clearly suggesting what follows. The speaker can mean that 30 minutes should be sufficient to do something completely or that he can do just a part of the plan. The important difference between ... *dake aru* and ... *shika nai* is that the former is not as suggestive, and the listener usually has to wait for the speaker to complete his sentence.

This difference is also true when money is involved. Saying *Juuman-en-shika arimasen-kara* means that the money is not enough to carry out a plan, while saying *Juuman-en-dake arimasu-kara* usually means that something can be done with the money, although what can be done is not yet clear.

When referring to your fluency in Japanese, if you want to emphasize that your knowledge of Japanese is small (regardless of how well you know it), you should say

*Nihongo-wa sukoshi-shika dekimasen.*

rather than *Nihongo-ga sukoshi-dake dekimasu.* Most Japanese will find the latter strange because they don't understand what you actually want to say.

(July 24, 1977)

ら」と言えば、相手はすぐ、時間が限られているから申し出は受け入れられない
のだと理解する。逆に「30分だけありますから」と言うと、時間がちょうど30
分あるというだけで、言外の意味は不明である。30分で何かを完了することが
できると言っているのかもしれないし、計画の一部のみ実行できると言っている
のかもしれない。

　「～だけある」と「～しかない」の大きな違いは、前者は後者のように残りの
部分を暗示しないので、文が終わるまで待たなければならない、ということであ
る。

　この違いは金の話についてもあてはまる。「10万円しかありませんから」と言
えば、計画を実行に移すのに十分な金がないということであり、「10万円だけあ
りますから」と言えば、ある程度のことはその金でできるという意味になるが、
それがどの程度かははっきりしない。

　日本語能力についても、自分の日本語が（実際にはどれほど堪能であったとし
ても）不十分であることを強調したい時には、

　　　日本語は少ししかできません

と言うべきである。「日本語が少しだけできます」と言うと、日本人のほうは、
実際には何を言おうとしているのかつかめず、変なことを言うと感じるであろ
う。

（1977.7.24）

# *Atsuku natta-n-desu-ne*
あつく なったんですね
*It has gotten hot, hasn't it?*

Mr. Lerner has been paying attention lately to how Japanese end their sentences and finds that they use *n-desu* at the end as much as *masu* and *desu*; in other words, they often say

*Itta-n-desu.*

(I went.)

rather than *Ikimashita* and

*Isogashii-n-desu.*

(I'm busy.)

rather than *Isogashii-desu.*

Yesterday morning he used this form and said to Mr. Takada,

*Atsuku natta-n-desu-ne.*

meaning "It has gotten hot, hasn't it?"

Mr. Takada hesitated for a moment before he said *Soo-desu-ne.* It was as if he was trying to find out what Mr. Lerner really meant.

After this, Mr. Lerner carefully listened to people talking about the weather, and found that they always say

*Atsuku narimashita-ne.*

or

# 暑くなったんですね

*It has gotten hot, hasn't it?*

　Mr. Lerner はこの頃、日本人が文の終わりにどんな言葉を使うかに注意しているが、それでわかったことは、「ます」「です」に劣らず、「〜んです」が多いということである。たとえば、「行きました」ではなく、

　　　行ったんです

とよく言うし、「いそがしいです」の代わりに、

　　　いそがしいんです

と言う。

　きのうの朝、Mr. Takada に会った時、この形を使って、

　　　暑クナッタンデスネ

とあいさつしてみた。

　Mr. Takada はちょっとためらってから「そうですね」と言った。どうやら Mr. Lerner の言ったことの真意がのみこめないようであった。

　このあと、天候についてのあいさつをよく聞いていると、みな必ず、

　　　暑くなりましたね
　　　きのうはよく降りましたね

とは言うが、絶対に「暑くなったんですね」「きのうはよく降ったんですね」と

*Kinoo-wa yoku furimashita-ne.*

(It rained a lot yesterday.)

but they never say *Atsuku natta-n-desu-ne* or *Kinoo-wa yoku futta-n-desu-ne* when they open a conversation by referring to the weather.

*　　　*　　　*

While *Atsuku narimashita-ne* simply states a fact, *Atsuku natta-n-desu-ne* presupposes a certain situation. The implication can vary; it can be that the speaker has noticed that someone, including the listener, has changed into summer clothes; it can be that someone looks tired from the heat or is having a cold drink. In other words, *Atsuku natta-n-desu-ne* can be paraphrased as "It's because it has gotten hot."

Sentences ending in *n-desu-ka* are not used in asking questions to start a conversation either unless there is a certain situation. For example, if you say to someone

*Isogashii-desu-ka.*

(Are you busy?)

you are simply asking whether he is busy or not. But if you say

*Isogashii-n-desu-ka.*

it can mean "Do you look tired because you are so busy?" "Are you so busy that you can't come with us to have a drink?" and so forth depending on the situation. Thus questions ending in *n-desu-ka* can imply various emotions such as concern, surprise, irritation, and criticism. If you ask them without the appropriate situation, the listener will be puzzled or even insulted.

(June 19, 1977)

は言わないのである……。

＊　　　　　＊　　　　　＊

　「暑くなりましたね」というのは、単に事実を叙述しているだけであるが、「暑くなったんですね」は、ある事態を前提としている。相手も含めてだれかが夏服に着がえたのに気がついたとか、だれかが暑さのせいで疲れた顔をしていたり、冷たい物を飲んでいたりしていたとか、言いかえれば、「暑くなったんですね」は、「それは暑くなったからですね」を縮めて言っているのである。

　「〜んですか」で終わる文は、特定の状況がない限り会話を始めるための質問には用いられない。だれかに、

　　　いそがしいですか

と聞くのは、単に相手が多忙か否かをたずねているのであるが、

　　　いそがしいんですか

と言うと、「いそがしいから疲れた顔をしていますか」とか「いそがしいから一緒に飲みに行けませんか」というような意味も持つ。「〜んですか」に終わる質問は、関心・驚き・焦慮・批判など、さまざまな感情を伝えがちである。適切な場面なしに「〜んですか」で質問すると、相手はとまどうか、時には気を悪くすることになる。

（1977.6.19）

# *Okutte-kimashita*
## 送ってきました
### He sent it to me

Mr. Lerner received a book from Mr. Kawakami yesterday. He wanted to tell Miss Yoshida about it in the office this morning. He said

*Kawakami-san-ga hon-o okurimashita.*

meaning "Mr. Kawakami sent me a book." He purposely left out *watashi-ni* (to me) because adding it would sound like a direct translation from English. But Miss Yoshida asked *Dare-ni?* (To whom?). Then, should Mr. Lerner have said *Kawakami-san-ga watashi-ni hon-o okurimashita*?

\*           \*           \*

Mr. Lerner should have said

*Kawakami-san-ga hon-o okutte-kimashita.*

Saying *Kawakami-san-ga hon-o okurimashita* sounds incomplete because it does not say to whom Mr. Kawakami sent the book. It is not natural to say *Kawakami-san-ga watashi-no hon-o okurimashita* either, because it sounds like a description of an action which has nothing to do with the speaker. In Japanese what directly concerns the speaker has to be expressed in a way different from describing what has happened to others. The English "to me" or "me" is very often expressed in phrases other than *watashi-ni* or *watashi-o.*

# 送ってきました

*He sent it to me*


　昨日 Mr. Kawakami から本が届いたので、Mr. Lerner はけさ会社で Miss Yoshida にさっそく知らせようと思い、

　　　川上サンガ本ヲ送リマシタ

と言った。「ワタシニ」を入れると英語の直訳のようになると思ったので、それは省いたのである。しかし Miss Yoshida は「だれに？」ときくではないか。では「ワタシニ本ヲ送リマシタ」と言うべきだったのだろうか……。

＊　　　　　＊　　　　　＊

　この場合は、

　　　川上さんが本を送ってきました

とすべきであった。「川上サンガ本ヲ送リマシタ」では、だれに送ったのか不明であるから、文としては不完全である。「川上サンガワタシニ本ヲ送リマシタ」も不自然である。それでは話し手と何も関係のない行為の叙述と聞こえるからである。日本語では、話し手に直接関係のあることは、他の人に起こったことの叙述とは異なる形をとる。英語の "to me" あるいは "me" に当たることが日本語では「ワタシニ」や「ワタシヲ」とは別の表現をとる。

　そうした表現のひとつは「動詞＋て」に「くる」をつける形である。「くる」は、だれかの行為が話し手に影響を及ぼすことを示す。何かが話し手に送られた

One of those phrases is to add *kuru* to the *-te* form of the verb; *kuru* indicates that someone's action affects the speaker. When something has been sent to the speaker, he says

*okutte-kimashita*
(he sent it to me)

instead of saying *watashi-ni okurimashita*. When referring to what has been said in someone's letter, the speaker says

*Kawakami-san-ga ii-to itte-kimashita.*
(Mr. Kawakami wrote to me that it is all right.)

In a similar way, instead of saying *Kawakami-san-ga watashi-ni denwa-o kakemashita*, one usually says

*Kawakami-san-ga denwa-o kakete-kimashita.*

to mean "Mr. Kawakami called me."

The following expressions with *kuru* are used very often in daily conversation.

*todokete-kimashita* (he delivered it to me)
*hakonde-kimashita* (he brought it to me)
*shirasete-kimashita* (he informed me of it)
*renraku-shite-kimashita* (he contacted me)

(July 22, 1979)

時は、「ワタシニ送リマシタ」ではなく、

　　　送ってきました

となる。手紙の中に書いてあることを伝える時に、

　　　川上さんがいいと言ってきました

のように言う。

　同じように、「川上サンガワタシニ電話ヲカケマシタ」と言わず、

　　　川上さんが電話をかけてきました

と言う。

　日常の話で「くる」がよく使われる例をあげれば次のようである。

　　　届けてきました
　　　運んできました
　　　知らせてきました
　　　連絡してきました

(1979.7.22)

# *Oishisoo-desu-ne*
## おいしそうですね
### It looks good

A few days ago Miss Yoshida brought to the office a cake she had made the previous day. The several people who gathered around the cake admired it lavishly before they ate it. Mr. Lerner also wanted to express his appreciation and said

*Oishiku miemasu-ne.*

meaning "It looks good." But Miss Yoshida didn't seem to be pleased and repeated *mieru?* in a somewhat displeased tone. Mr. Takada said that Mr. Lerner should have said

*Oishisoo-desu-ne.*

instead. He added that Mr. Lerner's sentence could imply that the cake was not as good as it looked.

*     *     *

. . . *soo* is added to various words and gives the meaning of ". . . looking." For instance, *oishii* means "delicious" while *oishisoo* means "delicious-looking"; *genkina hito* means "a healthy person" while *genkisoona hito* means "a person who looks healthy." When someone meets an acquaintance whom he has not seen for some time, he often greets him by saying

*Ogenkisoo-desu-ne.*

# おいしそうですね

### It looks good

　数日前のこと、Miss Yoshida が前日自分で作ったケーキを会社へ持ってきた。ケーキの周りに集まった数人の人々は、食べる前にさかんにケーキをほめた。Mr. Lerner も何か言ってほめようと思って、

　　　　オイシク見エマスネ

と言った。"It looks good." のつもりであったが、Miss Yoshida はよい顔をせず、やや不機嫌な口調で「見える？」と聞き直した。Mr. Takada は、

　　　　おいしそうですね

と言うべきだったのだと言った。Mr. Lerner の文は、見かけほどおいしくないという意味になりかねない、とも言った……。

　　　　　　　*　　　　　　　*　　　　　　　*

　「～そう」はさまざまな語につけて、「～に見える」の意味を表す。たとえば、「おいしそう」は「おいしい外観をもつ」の意味であり、「元気そうな人」は「元気な様子の人」の意味である。しばらくぶりで知人に会うと、

　　　　お元気そうですね

とか、

or

*Ogenkisoo-de, kekkoo-desu-ne.*

Both mean "I'm glad to see you looking fine."

Expressions with . . . *soo* usually do not imply that the appearance is different from the reality while expressions with *mieru* usually imply a difference between the appearance and the reality. Therefore, *yosasoo-desu-ne* simply means "it looks good" or "it sounds good," but *yoku miemasu-ne* usually implies that it won't be as good as it looks. Sometimes *mieru* is added to expressions ending in . . . *soo* as in *oishisoo-ni mieru* or *yosasoo-ni mieru*; these also often imply that the appearance is different from what the thing actually is.

Another . . . *soo* is added to the dictionary form of verbs, adjectives and others to mean "I heard . . ." Thus

*Furu-soo-desu.*

means "I heard that it's going to rain," while

*Furisoo-desu.*

means "It looks like it's going to rain." The difference between *u* and *i* preceding . . . *soo* makes quite a difference in meaning.

(September 10, 1978)

　　　お元気そうで、結構ですね

などとあいさつする。どちらも相手の元気な様子を喜ぶものである。

　「〜そう」のついた語句は、一般には外見と内容が異なるという意味をもたないが、「見える」は、外観と実際との違いをほのめかすのに使われるのが普通である。「よさそうですね」は単に「よいと思われる」の意味であるが、

　　　よく見えますね

は通常、見かけほどよくないという意味をもつ。「見える」は時には「〜そう」に加えて、「おいしそうに見える」とか「よさそうに見える」などと言う。この言いかたも、外見と中身の違いを意味することが多い。

　もうひとつの「〜そう」は動詞や形容詞などの辞書形（終止形）につくもので、「〜と聞いた」の意味を表す。

　　　降るそうです

は「降るということを聞いた」の意味であり、

　　　降りそうです

は、「降るように思われる」の意味である。「〜そう」に先立つ母音が "u" であるか "i" であるかによって、意味が全く違ってしまう。

（1978.9.10）

# *Hitoyama kudasai*
## ひとやま ください
### *Please give me one heap*

Last Friday evening Mr. Lerner dropped in at a fruit shop on his way home. He wanted some apples. There were several flat baskets with five or six apples piled up. He said to the woman in the store

*Ringo-o hitotsu kudasai.*

meaning "Please give me one (basket of) apples." But the woman looked embarrassed and said that she couldn't sell one apple alone. So he pointed to the basket and told her *Kore-o hitotsu kudasai* (lit., Please give one of this). Then she said

*Aa, hitoyama-desu-ka.*

and gave him the apples gladly.

Mr. Lerner felt that counting things in Japanese is quite difficult. He had learned several counters already but he seemed to have some more to learn.

*       *        *

Most objects are counted as *hitotsu, futatsu, mittsu* (one, two, three), etc., but there are several counters used depending on the shape of things. Thin objects like paper are counted with *-mai*, and thin, long objects like pencils are counted as *ippon, nihon, sanbon*, etc. One student who is tall

# ひとやま下さい

## *Please give me one heap*

先週の金曜日の夕方、Mr. Lerner は帰り道にくだもの屋に立ち寄った。りんごを買おうと思って見ると、平たいかごに5、6個のりんごを積んだものがいくつか置いてあった。そこで、店番の女性に、

リンゴヲヒトツ下サイ

と言った。「ひとつのかごのりんご」のつもりであったが、女性は困った顔をして、1個だけ売るわけにはいかないと言った。そこでかごを指して「これをひとつ下さい」と言ってみたら、

ああ、ひとやまですか

と言って、喜んでりんごを渡してくれた。

日本語で物を数えるのはむずかしいものだと、Mr. Lerner は感じた。物を数える言葉をすでにいくつか習ったが、まだまだ習わなければいけないようである……。

＊　　　　　＊　　　　　＊

大抵の物体は「ひとつ、ふたつ、みっつ……」と数えるが、形によって異なる助数詞を用いる場合がある。薄い、紙のような物は「〜枚」と数え、鉛筆のような細長い物は「1本、2本、3本……」と数える。かつて背が高くてやせた学生が、ぼくみたいな人間は「1本」でしょうかと質問したことがある。いや、人間

and slender once wondered if people like him should be counted with *ippon*. No, human beings are counted with *hitori, futari, sannin*, etc., regardless of how big or small they are. On the other hand, small animals are counted with *-hiki* while big ones are counted with *-too*.

In addition to these counters, there are some used for collections of things. When things are piled up, *-yama* is used, as in *hitoyama, futayama*; when the container is a plate, things piled up on it are counted as *hitosara* (one plate); things contained in boxes are counted with *-hako*.

Counters are now in the process of being simplified; traditional counters are now often replaced by more simple counters like *hitotsu, futatsu*, etc., or *ikko, niko* (one piece, two pieces). For example, two different counters have been used for two classical Japanese instruments, the *koto* and *shamisen*, but nowadays many young people use *hitotsu* or *ikko* for either of them.

It is good to be able to use some basic counters such as *-mai, -hon, -satsu* (used for counting books), *hitori, -dai* (for vehicles and machines), *-ken* (for houses). It is also recommended that you know that words signifying number are usually used like adverbs. Namely, to say that you want one heap of apples, rather than saying

*Hitoyama-no ringo-o kudasai.*

it is more conversational to say

*Ringo-o hitoyama kudasai.*

(October 15, 1978)

は、体が大きくても小さくても関係なく、「1人、2人、3人……」である。ところが動物は、小さいのは「〜ひき」で、大きいのは「〜頭」と数える。

　こうした助数詞の他に、物の集合を数える言葉もある。盛り上げた物は「ひとやま、ふたやま」のように「〜やま」で数えるが、入れ物が皿であれば盛った物は「〜さら」となるし、箱に入れた物は「〜はこ」で数える。

　助数詞は次第に簡略化していく傾向にあり、伝統的な助数詞に代わって、簡単なもの、つまり「ひとつ、ふたつ」あるいは「1個、2個」のようなものが使われることが多くなった。たとえば日本の古典的な楽器の場合など、琴と三味線では別の数えかたをしていたが、最近の若い人は、どちらも「ひとつ」あるいは「1個」と言う人が多くなった。

　「枚」「本」「冊」「ひとり」「台」「軒」など、基本的なものは、使えることが望ましい。また、数を示す語は通常副詞的に使われるということも、知っておくとよいと思われる。すなわち、りんごのやまを買う時、

　　　ひとやまのりんごを下さい

と言うより、

　　　りんごをひとやま下さい

と言うほうが、会話として自然なのである。

(1978.10.15)

# *Kowashite-arimasu*
## こわしてあります
### *Someone has broken it*

Mr. Lerner recently learned a new grammatical rule: he was told that a transitive verb plus *te-arimasu* means the same thing as an intransitive verb plus *te-imasu*; namely, both *mado-ga akete-arimasu* and *mado-ga aite-imasu* mean "the window is open." He wanted to use this expression in actual conversation some time. Yesterday morning when he tried to turn on the reading lamp on his desk at the office, he noticed that it didn't work, so he showed it to Miss Yoshida and told her

*Kowashite-arimasu-ne.*

to mean "it's broken." He thought that was just the same as *Kowarete-imasu-ne*, but Miss Yoshida didn't understand. She said that he should say *Kowarete-imasu-ne* instead.

*       *         *       *         *

It is often explained as a grammatical rule that the two expressions—a transitive verb plus *te-arimasu* and an intransitive verb plus *te-imasu*—are used in the same way. According to this, the expressions in the two groups below mean the same thing:

**Group 1**

*aite-imasu* ( < *aku*, v.i.)

*shimatte-imasu* ( < *shimaru*, v.i.)

*denki-ga tsuite-imasu* ( < *tsuku*, v.i.)

# こわしてあります

*Someone has broken it*

　最近 Mr. Lerner は文法の規則をひとつ習った。それは、「他動詞＋てあります」は「自動詞＋ています」と同じ意味になるということで、「窓があけてあります」と「窓があいています」はともに、"The window is open." の意味になる、というのである。Mr. Lerner はこの表現をいつか実際の会話で使ってみたいと思っていた。昨日の朝、会社の机の上のスタンドをつけようとしたが、故障しているのがわかったので、そのスタンドを Miss Yoshida に見せて、

　　　コワシテアリマスネ

と言った。"It's broken" の意味のつもりで、「こわれていますね」と同じことだと思ったのだが、Miss Yoshida には通じなかった。彼女は「こわれていますね」と言わなくてはいけないと言った……。

＊　　　　　　＊　　　　　　＊

　2つの表現——「他動詞＋てあります」と「自動詞＋ています」——は、同じように用いられると説明されることが多い。この説明に従えば、以下の2群の表現は同じことを言っていることになる。

**第1群**
あいています　（＜あく〔自動詞〕）
しまっています　（＜しまる〔自動詞〕）
電気がついています　（＜つく〔自動詞〕）

**Group 2**

*akete-arimasu* ( < *akeru*, v.t.) (it's open)

*shimete-arimasu* ( < *shimeru*, v.t.) (it's closed)

*denki-ga tsukete-arimasu* ( < *tsukeru*, v.t.) (the light is on)

It is true that the two types of expressions are used to describe the same state of things, but the speaker's mental attitude towards this state of things is different. In this sense, the two expressions should not be regarded as the same. While expressions in group 1 are used to describe the state of things just as they are, expressions in group 2 imply that someone has done the action purposely, and they often imply the speaker's surprise, criticism, reprimand, or other such feelings. Miss Yoshida didn't understand when Mr. Lerner said *Kowashite-arimasu-ne* because that implied that he was blaming someone for purposely damaging his reading lamp.

This contrast is, however, not applied to all verbs. Some verbs do not have corresponding transitive or intransitive verbs, and sometimes the *te-arimasu* form cannot be used because the meaning would be strange. For instance, you can say *Mise-ga narande-imasu* (Several stores are line up), but you cannot say *Mise-ga narabete-arimasu* (Someone has lined up the stores).

(July 13, 1980)

第2群

あけてあります　（＜あける〔他動詞〕）

しめてあります　（＜しめる〔他動詞〕）

**電気がつけてあります**　（＜つける〔他動詞〕）

　この2つの群の表現が同じ状態を描くのに使われていることは事実である。しかし、その状態に対する話し手の心的態度は異なっている。この意味では、2つの表現は同一であるとは言いがたい。第1群の表現は事態を単にあるがままに報じているのに対し、第2群の表現はだれかがその行為を意図的に行ったことをほのめかし、話し手の驚き、批判、非難などの感情を暗示している。Mr. Lerner が「コワシテアリマスネ」と言った時 Miss Yoshida が理解しなかったのは、だれかが故意にスタンドをこわしたと非難している感じがしたからである。

　しかし、すべての動詞についてこうした対比が生じるわけではない。動詞によっては対応する他動詞ないし自動詞をもたないものもあるし、「〜てあります」を使うと意味をなさなくなってしまうものもある。たとえば「店が並んでいます」とは言えるが、「店が並べてあります」とは言えない。

（1980.7.13）

# *Ichido ome-ni kakaritai-to omoimasu*
## 一度 お目に かかりたいと 思います
### *I'd like to see you sometime*

A Mr. Kimura called Mr. Lerner on the phone yesterday afternoon; he said that he was working on a certain project and wondered if Mr. Lerner could help him. After explaining the situation, he said

*Ichido ome-ni kakaritai-to omoimasu-ga . . .*
(lit., I'd like to see you one time, but . . .)

Mr. Lerner told him when he would be available and hung up the phone, but he wondered why Mr. Kimura had said *Ichido . . .* (One time . . .) Did he want to see Mr. Lerner just once and no more?

*          *          *

The word *ichido* is often used to mean "sometime in the future" when making a proposal or request in a social situation. *Ichido ome-ni kakaritai* does not mean that the speaker is determined not to see the listener more than once. Rather, saying

*Zehi ichido oide-kudasai.*

means "Please come and see me by all means" or "You must come and see me sometime."

In a similar way *hitotsu* is also used to mean "some" when offering something or making a proposal as in

# 一度お目にかかりたいと思います

*I'd like to see you sometime*

　きのうの午後、Mr. Kimura という人から電話があって、ある企画に関して Mr. Lerner の助けを得たいがと言ってきた。事情を説明したあと、その人は、

　　一度お目にかかりたいと思いますが……

と言った。都合のつく日時を答えて電話を切ったが、なぜ「一度」と言ったのだろうと Mr. Lerner は思った。一度だけ会えばもう会わないつもりなのだろうか……。

＊　　　　＊　　　　＊

　「一度」という語は、人に対して提案や依頼をする時、「将来のある時」の意味でよく使われる。「一度お目にかかりたい」というのは、二度と会わない決心をしているということではない。

　　ぜひ一度おいでください

というのは、「ぜひ会いに来てください」とか「いつか必ず会いに来てほしい」の意味である。

　同じように「ひとつ」も、物をすすめ提案したりする場合には、「少し」の意味に用いられる。たとえば、

*Hitotsu oagari-kudasai.*
(Please have some.)

This *hitotsu* is also used in a request as in

*Hitotsu onegai-shimasu.*

meaning "Please take care of this. Thank you." Sometimes a person who accepts a request will say

*Ja, hitotsu yatte-mimashoo.*
(Then I'll give it a try.)

These words *ichido* and *hitotsu* can be left out as far as the meaning is concerned, but they serve the function of making the intention of the following speech clear at the beginning of the sentence, so the listener can get ready. The use of this kind of word is especially recommended in social situations; it will help avoid having your Japanese sound abrupt.

(January 3, 1982)

# *Sono-uchi*
## そのうち
### By and by

Mr. Okada came to discuss some business with Mr. Lerner the other day, and when he was leaving after the discussions, he said he had some

　　　ひとつおあがりください

のように言う。この「ひとつ」は依頼の場合にも

　　　ひとつお願いします

のように用いられる。時には依頼に応じた人が、

　　　じゃ、ひとつやってみましょう

と答えたりする。

　このような「一度」や「ひとつ」は、意味の上ではなくてもよいわけであるが、文の最初にこれから言おうとすることを明らかにし、聞き手にそれに対する心がまえをさせるという働きがある。この種の表現は人づきあいの場では特に大切で、ぶっきらぼうな日本語と思われないためには必要なものである。

(1982.1.3)

# そのうち

## By and by

　この間 Mr. Okada が Mr. Lerner のもとへ商談にやってきたが、帰る時、ちょっと Miss Yoshida にたずねたいことがあると言った。だが彼女はちょうど外へ

thing to ask Miss Yoshida, but she had just stepped out of the office. Mr. Lerner suggested that Mr. Okada have a cup of coffee and wait for her, adding

*Chikai uchi-ni modotte-kimasu-kara.*

meaning "Because she will be back very soon." Mr. Okada agreed, saying

*Ee, sono-uchi mieru-deshoo.*
(Yes, she will show up pretty soon.)

Mr. Lerner wondered if he was wrong when he said *chikai uchi-ni*; he had learned that *uchi* is used to refer to a time interval, and he thought that both *chikai uchi-ni* and *sono uchi-ni* meant "before long," but he didn't know the difference between the two.

*      *      *

Mr. Lerner's sentence sounded strange because *chikai uchi-ni* cannot be used to refer to something that will happen during the same day. Although it does not specify the time, it usually refers to things that are likely to take place after a few days of after a few weeks or months, and not after a few minutes.

On the other hand, *sono-uchi(-ni)* is used to refer more indefinitely to the future. It can be used for what will happen after a few minutes as in Mr. Okada's remark about Miss Yoshida's coming back. It is also used to refer to what will happen after a fairly long time as in

*Sono uchi-ni keeki-mo kaifuku-suru-deshoo.*
(Business will improve one of these days.)

Because of this indefiniteness, *sono uchi(-ni)* is often used in social situations as in

出ていたので、Mr. Lerner は、コーヒーでも飲んで待っているようにすすめ、

　　　　近イウチニモドッテキマスカラ

とつけ加えた。Mr. Okada は同意し、

　　　　ええ、そのうち見えるでしょう

と言った。

　自分が「近イウチニ」と言ったのは間違いだったのだろうか、と Mr. Lerner は思った。「うち」は時の隔たりをさし、「近いうちに」も「そのうち」も「間もなく」の意味だと思っていたので、2つの表現の違いがわからなかった……。

＊　　　　　＊　　　　　＊

　Mr. Lerner の文が奇異にひびいたのは、「近いうちに」は同じ日のうちに起こることについては使えないからである。時間を特に限ってはいないが、一般に2、3日のち、あるいは2、3週間、2、3か月ののちに起こるようなことに用い、2、3分あとのことについては使わない。

　一方、「そのうち(に)」は、もっと漠然とした将来について用いられる。Mr. Okada が Miss Yoshida の帰りについて言ったように、数分のちのことでも使うことができる。時にはかなり長い時間のあとで起こることについても用いられる。たとえば、

　　　　そのうちに景気も回復するでしょう

のような場合である。

　こうした意味の広さから、「そのうち(に)」は人づきあいの場でもよく用いられる。

A: *Doozo ichido oasobi-ni oide-kudasai.*

(Please come to see us.)

B: *Arigatoo-gozaimasu. Izure sono-uchi-ni.*

(Thank you. I will come sometime.)

(February 1, 1981)

# *Takada-san-tachi*
## 高田さんたち
### Mr. Takada and others

Mr. Lerner was invited to Miss Yoshida's house last Saturday. When he arrived at her house she met him at the door and said

*Takada-san-tachi-mo kite-imasu.*

(lit., The Takada people also came and are here.)

Mr. Lerner thought that Mr. Takada had brought his wife and children, but only Mr. Takada and his colleagues were there.

Then Mr. Lerner remembered that . . . *tachi* often means ". . . and others," and realized that Miss Yoshida had referred to Mr. Takada and others by *Takada-san-tachi*. Incidentally, he also remembered that when he first learned the word *tachi*, he made a mistake in using it; when addressing an envelope to the Takadas, he wrote

*Takada-tachi-san*

A：どうぞ一度お遊びにおいでください

B：ありがとうございます。いずれそのうちに

などが、その例である。

(1981.2.1)

# 高田さんたち

## Mr. Takada and others

　先週の土曜日 Mr. Lerner は Miss Yoshida の家へ招かれて行った。家に着くと彼女が玄関に出迎えて、

　　高田さんたちも来ています

と言った。Mr. Lerner は、Mr. Takada が奥さんや子供たちをつれて来たのだと思った。しかし中へ入ってみると Mr. Takada と同僚しかいなかった。

　そこで思い出したのは、「〜たち」というのは「〜とその他の人」の意味になることがある、ということだった。Miss Yoshida の言った「高田さんたち」の「たち」はその意味だったのだ。そのついでに思い出したのだが、「たち」という語をはじめて学んだ時、使いかたを誤って、高田夫妻に出す手紙に、

　　タカダタチサン

と書いたことがある。その話をすると Miss Yoshida は大笑いした……。

to mean "Mr. and Mrs. Takada." Miss Yoshida laughed a lot when he told her about it.

\*       \*       \*

*Tachi* is added to words meaning a person or to the name of a person and forms a word which indicates either that there are more than one person or that people of the same kind are included. For instance, *gakusee-tachi* can mean either "students" or "students and their like." When *tachi* is added to names, it is more likely that the word indicates people of the same kind; thus *Takada-san-tachi* usually means "Mr. Takada and members of his group."

If Miss Yoshida had been referring to the Takada family, she would have said *Takada-san-to okusan-to kodomo-san-tachi* (Mr. Takada, his wife, and his children). If just Mr. and Mrs. Takada had been there, she would have said *Takada-san-to okusan*. In formal speech, one sometimes says *Takada-fusai* to mean "Mr. and Mrs. Takada."

*Tachi* can be added to pronouns for such words as *watashi-tachi* (we), *anata-tachi* (you) and *ano-hito-tachi* (they), although these words are not used as often as their English equivalents.

Another thing one has to keep in mind is that *tachi* does not imply politeness. When you want to be polite, you should use *gata* in place of *tachi* as in *anata-gata* (you), *sensee-gata* (professors), *okosan-gata* (your children), and so forth. When referring to the members of one's own group, it is modest to say *watashi-domo* instead of *watashi-tachi*.

(Februaly 10, 1980)

\*　　　　\*　　　　\*

「たち」は人や人名を表す語につけて、人がひとりでないこと、あるいは同じような人が含まれていることを示す。たとえば「学生たち」と言えば、「複数の学生」あるいは「学生やそのような人々」の意味になる。「たち」が人名についた時は同じような人を示す可能性が高い。「高田さんたち」と言えば、通常「高田さんとそのグループの人」のことである。

「高田一家」のことをさすのであれば、Miss Yoshida は「高田さんと奥さんと子供さんたち」と言ったであろう。Mr. Takada と Mrs. Takada だけであったら、「高田さんと奥さん」と言ったであろう。改まった場面では「高田夫妻」ということもある。

「たち」は代名詞にもついて「わたしたち」「あなたたち」「あの人たち」のようにも使われるが、こうした語は英語の場合にくらべて使われる頻度が低い。

もうひとつ気をつけるべきことは、「たち」は丁寧な話しかたには使えないということである。丁寧に話すには「たち」の代わりに「がた」をつけて、「あなたがた」「先生がた」「お子さんがた」などとする。身内の者について言う時は「わたしたち」と言うより「わたしども」と言うほうが謙虚とされる。

(1980.2.10)

# *Tekitoo-ni yatte-kudasai*
## てきとうに やってください
### Please use your own judgment

While Mr. Lerner and Mr. Takada were talking during a break in their work, Miss Yoshida came to ask Mr. Takada some questions about the typing he had asked her to do. Mr. Takada answered several specific questions, and then said

*Ato-wa tekitoo-ni yatte-kudasai.*
(lit., As for the rest, please do it properly.)

Miss Yoshida said that she understood and left them. Mr. Lerner wondered what the expression *tekitoo-ni* means exactly, and also wondered why she had gone back to her work without asking any further questions.

*       *       *

The word *tekitoo* usually means "appropriate," as in such expressions as *tekitoona kotoba* (appropriate words) or *tekitoona hito* (suitable person). But in a situation as mentioned above, *Tekitoo-ni yatte-kudasai* or *Tekitoo-ni onegai-shimasu* means "Please do it in the way you think is appropriate," and actually implies that the speaker leaves it to the judgment of the listener.

Suppose someone asks you to plan a party to celebrate the anniversary of the founding of the company, and tells you the amount of money you can spend and the names of the people to be invited. When you ask him

# 適当にやってください

*Please use your own judgment*

Mr. Lerner と Mr. Takada が休憩時間に雑談しているところへ Miss Yoshida が来て、Mr. Takada の頼んだタイプのことについて質問した。Mr. Takada はいくつかの具体的な質問に答えたのち、

あとは適当にやってください

と言った。

Miss Yoshida は了承して去った。Mr. Lerner は「適当に」というのは正確にはどういう意味だろう、また Miss Yoshida がそれ以上のことをきかずにもどっていったのはなぜだろうと思った……。

＊　　　　　＊　　　　　＊

「適当」という語は通常、「適当な言葉」や「適当な人」のように、妥当性が高いという意味に用いる。しかし上記のように、「適当にやってください」とか「適当にお願いします」という場合は、「自分がちょうどよいと思うようにやってください」という意味で、実際には相手の裁量にことをゆだねるという気持ちを示している。

たとえば、会社の創立記念日を祝うためのパーティーを計画してほしいと、だれかに頼まれたとする。そして、その際、費してよい金額と招待者の名簿を渡されたとする。そのうち飲み物に使うのはどのくらいの割合か、食べ物についてはどうかとたずねた場合、頼んだ人は、

what portion of money should go for drinks and what portion for food, he may say

*Sore-wa tekitoo-ni yatte-kudasai.*

meaning that the matter is left to you.

There still remains a question as to what extent you can use your own judgment. When saying *tekitoo-ni* the speaker usually has some idea of how the work should be carried out, and doesn't expect you to do things in a way completely different from his idea. You will check the previous cases and try not to deviate too much from them.

Thus the expression *tekitoo-ni* can be used in this way only in situations where the speaker and the listener share the same understanding. Even among Japanese sometimes the listener has a difficult time sensing what the speaker actually expects of him. And this expression is usually used by a speaker to someone who is not superior to him because it is impolite for him to expect his superior to sense his intentions.

(June 29, 1980)

# *Sassoku*
## さっそく
### *Right away*

Mr. Lerner has come to be able to use various expressions pretty well, but still sometimes uses them inappropriately. Just yesterday he called an

　　　それは適当にやってください

と言うかもしれない。

　それにしても、どの程度まで自分の裁量で決めてよいのかという疑問は残る。「適当に」と頼んだ人は大抵、どうやってほしいかだいたいの心づもりがあるのであって、自分の考えと全く違う方法でやってもらおうとは思っていない。頼まれたほうは、前例を検討して、あまり逸脱しないように気をつけることになる。

　このように、「適当にやってくれ」と言えるのは、頼むほうと頼まれるほうが同じ考えをもっている場合に限られる。日本人同士でも、頼まれたほうは、相手が何を期待しているのか察しをつけるために苦労することもある。この「適当にやって」という表現は通常、自分のより目上の人には使わない。目上の人に自分の意図を察してほしいと期待するのは礼儀に外れるからである。

(1980.6.29)

# さっそく

*Right away*

　Mr. Lerner は、いろいろな日本語の表現がかなり使えるようになったが、まだ使いかたの不適切な場合もある。昨日も、新しいテレビの具合を見てもらうため

electric appliance store to have them check his new TV set. He had bought it recently but somehow or other it didn't work right, so he said

*Terebi-ga sassoku kowarete-shimatta-n-desu.*

to mean "It broke right away." The man just said

*Sassoku ukagaimasu.*
(I'll come right away.)

but Miss Yoshida laughed. She said his sentence was funny because *sassoku* is used when a person is going to do something. Then Mr. Takada disagreed saying that it is all right to say

*Sassoku henji-ga kimashita.*
(The reply came right away.)

\*　　　　\*　　　　\*

Among various words meaning "soon" or "right away," *sugu* is used in many different cases. Mr. Lerner could have said *Sugu kowaremashita* and the man could have said *Sugu ukagaimasu.* On the other hand, *sassoku* is more limited in use; it is used when referring to a person's actions when the person is willing to do that action. Thus when someone means he will come right away to help someone else, he will say *Sassoku ukagaimasu* to imply that he is ready and willing to do so.

Therefore *Terebi-ga sassoku kowaremashita* cannot be used because a TV set has no intentions of its own. In the case of *Henji-ga sassoku kimashita,* the action of sending a reply is done by a person by his will. You cannot usually say

*Sassoku ame-ga furimashita.*
(It rained right away.)

電気器具店に電話した時、つい最近買ったばかりなのになぜか調子がわるいので、

　　　テレビガサッソクコワレテシマッタンデス

と言った。店員はただ、

　　　さっそくうかがいます

と言っただけだったが、Miss Yoshida は Mr. Lerner の文はおかしいと笑い、「さっそく」を使うのは人間が何かする時だけだと言った。すると Mr. Takada が、

　　　さっそく返事が来ました

と言うじゃないか、と横やりを入れた……。

＊　　　　　　　＊　　　　　　　＊

　"soon" "right away" の意味を表すいくつかの語のうち、「すぐ」はいろいろな場面で使われる。Mr. Lerner も「すぐこわれました」と言ってもよかったし、店員も「すぐうかがいます」と言ってもよかったわけである。それに対し「さっそく」は用法が限られており、だれか人がこころよくその行為をとるという場合に用いられる。だれかの手助けをするためにかけつける時など、こころよく助けに来るつもりであることを示すために、「さっそくうかがいます」と言う。

　　したがって、「テレビガサッソクコワレマシタ」とは、テレビには自己の意志がないから言うことができない。「返事がさっそく来ました」と言えるのは、返答を送ることが人の意志によって行われたことだからである。通常、

　　　さっそく雨がふりました

or

> *Sassoku kuraku narimashita.*
> (It became dark right away.)

unless you're personifying nature.

> You can say

> *Sassoku kusuri-o nomimashita.*
> (I took the medicine right away.)

but you cannot say *Sassoku naorimashita* to mean "I became better very soon," because it is not within your will to become better.

(March 9, 1980)

# *Joozu-ni natte-ikimashita*
## じょうずに なっていきました
### It kept on improving

Mr. Lerner noticed that Miss Yoshida's English had improved quite rapidly, so he remarked to Mr. Takada the other day

> *Yoshida-san-no eego-wa joozu-ni natte-ikimashita-ne.*

meaning "Miss Yoshida's English has improved." Mr. Takada agreed, but corrected his sentence to

> *. . . joozu-ni natte-kimashita.*

　　さっそく暗くなりました

などとは、自然を擬人化しない限り言うことができない。

　　さっそく薬をのみました

とは言えるが、「すぐよくなった」の意味で、「さっそく治りました」とは言えない。病気の回復は意志の力で左右することはできないからである。

(1980.3.9)

# 上手になっていきました

## *It kept on improving*

　Miss Yoshida の英語が急速に進歩したのに気づいた Mr. Lerner は、この間 Mr. Takada に、

　　吉田サンノ英語ハ上手ニナッテイキマシタネ

と言った。Mr. Takada はその通りだとは答えたが、文としては、

　　……上手になってきました

Mr. Lerner had thought that both . . . *te-iku* and . . . *te-kuru* were used to mean "keep . . . ing," and had not learned the difference between the two.

*       *       *

While . . . *te-kuru* is used to refer to an action approaching the speaker, . . . *te-iku* refers to an action going away from him. Therefore, a change up to the present is usually described with . . . *te-kuru* as in

*Samuku natte-kimashita.*
(It has become cold.)
*Eego-ga joozu-ni natte-kimashita.*
(Her English has improved.)
*Bukka-ga agatte-kimashita.*
(Things have become more expensive.)

And . . . *te-iku* is used most often to refer to a change continuing into the future as in

*Kore-kara samuku natte-ikimasu.*
(It will become colder from now on.)
*Bukka-ga agatte-iku-deshoo.*
(Things will become more and more expensive.)

Since . . . *te-iku* implies that an action or state of things is going away from the speaker, it is appropriate to use it to refer to the future in conversation, but it is also used to refer to the past in written sentences where the writer is supposed to be detached from the action or the state of things that he is writing about. For instance, to describe how Japan was modernized in the Meiji period;

*Nihon-wa kooshite shidai-ni kindaika-shite-itta.*
(In this way Japan was gradually modernized.)

でなければおかしいと言った。

　Mr. Lerner は、「～ていく」も「～てくる」もどちらも「～しつづける」(keep . . . ing) の意味だと思っていたので、両者の違いを人にきいたことがなかったのである……。

*　　　　　*　　　　　*

　「～てくる」は話し手のほうに向かって行われる行為をさし、「～ていく」は話し手から離れていく行為をさす。したがって、現在までの変化については、「～てくる」が普通で、

> 寒くなってきました
> 英語が上手になってきました
> 物価が上がってきました

のように言う。

　「～ていく」は、将来に向かって続く行為について用いられることが多い。たとえば、

> これから寒くなっていきます
> 物価が上がっていくでしょう

のように用いられる。

　「～ていく」は、ある行為なり状態なりが話し手から遠ざかることを意味するので、会話では将来について使うのが適切であるが、書いたものでは過去を表すこともある。これは書き言葉では、書き手は自分の述べている行為や状況から離れた立場をとるからである。たとえば、明治時代の日本がいかに近代化したかを描写する時など、

> 日本はこうして次第に近代化していった

のように書く。

Or, referring to the hero of his novel, an author may write

*Kare-wa sono kesshin-o tsuyomete-itta.*

(He was more and more determined to do so.)

This use of . . . *te-iku* is often seen in textbooks or literary writings because it implies the detached attitude of the writer.

(December 14, 1980)

# *Sen-en-mo daseba . . .*
## 千円も 出せば…
*If you pay 1,000 yen . . .*

Mr. Lerner noticed that Mr. Takada had a new lighter. Since it was a very stylish one, he complimented him on it. Miss Yoshida also noticed it, admired it, and asked if it was very expensive. Mr. Takada replied no, and added

*Sen-en-mo daseba doko-demo kaemasu-yo.*

(You can buy it anywhere if you pay 1,000 yen.)

Then Miss Yoshida said

*Sen-en-mo suru-n-desu-ka.*

(Does it cost as much as 1,000 yen?)

Mr. Takada smiled and said that she knew very little about the cost of lighters. And Mr. Lerner wondered whether the two *mo*s used by Mr.

あるいは、小説の中の主人公について、作家は、

　　　彼はその決心を強めていった

のように書く。

　このような「〜ていく」の用法は、筆者の超越的な立場を示す教科書や文芸作品などに往々にしてみられる。

(1980.12.14)

# 千円も出せば…

## *If you pay 1,000 yen . . .*

　Mr. Lerner は、Mr. Takada が新しいライターを持っているのを見た。なかなかしゃれたライターだったので、それをほめた。Miss Yoshida も見て感心し、高かったでしょうねと言った。Mr. Takada はそんなことはないと答え、

　　　千円も出せばどこでも買えますよ

と言った。すると Miss Yoshida は、

　　　千円もするんですか

と言った。Mr. Takada は笑って、ライターの値段を知らないんだなと答えた。それにしても、Mr. Takada の使った「も」と Miss Yoshida の使った「も」は同じものか別のものか、Mr. Lerner にはわからなかった……。

Takada and Miss Yoshida were the same or different.

*      *      *

The particle *mo* added to words indicating amounts implies the speaker's evaluation of the amount. For instance, *sen-en-mo* can mean either "only 1,000 yen" or "as much as 1,000 yen." Mr. Takada used it, in the conversation above, to mean "only 1,000 yen," because he felt that 1,000 yen was a small amount to pay for a lighter. On the other hand, Miss Yoshida said *sen-en-mo* to imply that 1,000 yen seemed to her a large amount of money for a lighter.

Whether *mo* is used positively or negatively is decided by the context. Very often, when followed by . . . *eba* (if . . .), *mo* means "only." Suppose several people are waiting for someone who is late and wondering if they should stop waiting. Someone may suggest waiting a little longer, saying

*Ato go-fun-mo mateba kuru-deshoo.*

(He should show up in five minutes.)

In this case the speaker implies that five minutes is rather short. But *mo* means "as much as" when someone says angrily

*Go-fun-mo matta-noni kimasen-deshita.*

(Although I waited for five minutes, he never showed up.)

About learning Japanese, a teacher may say to a student

*Ni-nen-mo yareba joozu-ni narimasu.*

(You will become good at it if you study for just two years.)

and the student may say

*Ni-nen-mo yaru-n-desu-ka!*

(Do I have to study it for two whole years!?)

(August 23, 1981)

＊　　　　　＊　　　　　＊

　数量を表す語のあとにつけた「も」は、話し手の評価を映し出している。たとえば「千円も」は「わずか千円」の意味にもなり「千円という高額」の意味にもなり得る。上記の話で Mr. Takada が使った「も」は「わずか千円」の意味である。彼としてはライターの値段としては千円は極めて少額だと感じていたわけである。それに対して Miss Yoshida はライターに千円とは高額だという気持ちで、「千円も」と言ったのである。

　「も」が積極的な意味をもつか否定的な意味をもつかは、文脈によって決まる。あとに「～ば」がつくと、「も」が「わずか」の意味になることが多い。たとえば、何人かの人がおくれてくる人を待っているとする。もうそろそろ待たないで出かけようかと考え始めたころ、だれかが、もう少し待つことを提案する目的で、

　　　あと５分も待てば来るでしょう

と言うかもしれない。この場合話し手は５分は短い時間だと言っている。しかし、だれかが怒った口調で、

　　　５分も待ったのに来ませんでした

と言った場合、「も」は「多くの」の意味をもつ。

　日本語の学習に関して、教師は学習者に、

　　　２年もやれば上手になります

と言うかもしれないが、学習者のほうは、

　　　２年もやるんですか！

と言うかもしれない。

(1981.8.23)

# *Hareru yoona ki-ga shimasu*
## 晴れる ような 気が します
### I have a feeling it's going to clear up

It was raining hard yesterday morning but by lunch time it wasn't raining as hard. Someone wondered if it would keep raining through the evening. Mr. Takada said

> *Kyoo-wa furu-to omoimasu-ne.*
> (I think it will rain all day today.)

Then Miss Yoshida disagreed, saying

> *Watashi-wa hareru yoona ki-ga shimasu-kedo.*
> (lit., I have a feeling that it will clear up, but.)

Mr. Lerner had heard the expression . . . *ki-ga suru* before, but now he thought about the difference between . . . *to omou* and . . . *yoona ki-ga suru*, and wondered which sounds more definite.

*      *      *

There are various expressions with *ki* such as *ki-ga suru, ki-ni naru, ki-ga tsuku*, etc. *Ki-ga suru* literally means "I have a feeling," and sometimes is added to adjectives as in *iyana ki-ga suru* (I feel it's unpleasant), *zannenna ki-ga suru* (I feel it's regrettable), or *donna ki-ga shimasu-ka* (how do you feel about it?). But the more common usage is to express one's opinion in a reserved way and for this purpose it usually follows *yoona* as in *hareru*

# 晴れるような気がします

*I have a feeling it's going to clear up*

　昨日は朝のうちはひどい雨であったが、昼ごろには少しおさまってきていた。だれかが夕方までは降りつづくかなと言いだした。Mr. Takada はそれを聞いて、

　　　きょうは降ると思いますね

と言った。ところが Miss Yoshida は反対で、

　　　わたしは晴れるような気がしますけど

と言った。

　この「〜気がする」という表現は、Mr. Lerner も聞いたことがあったが、「〜と思う」と「〜ような気がする」の違いを考え始めたら、どちらのほうが確実性が高いのかわからなくなった……。

　　　　　　　＊　　　　　　　＊　　　　　　　＊

　「気」を使った表現は、「気がする」「気になる」「気がつく」など、いろいろある。「気がする」は文字通りには「そう感じる」ということで、時にはこの前に形容する言葉をつけて「いやな気がする」「残念な気がする」「どんな気がしますか」などと使う。しかしもっと頻繁に使われるのは、自分の意見を控えめに表すという用法で、この場合は「晴れるような気がします」のように「ような」をつけて用いる。「〜ような気がする」は「〜と思う」よりは確実性が低い。たとえばだれかが姿を現すかどうか言い合っている時、

*yoona ki-ga suru.* Saying . . . *yoona ki-ga suru* sounds less definite than
. . . *to omou.* For instance, when discussing whether someone is coming,
saying

> *Kyoo kuru-to omoimasu.*
> (I think he will come today.)

sounds as if the speaker has some reason to believe that the person will
come, while saying

> *Kyoo kuru yoona ki-ga shimasu.*

implies that the speaker doesn't have any definite reason to think so.

Very often *nan-to-naku* (for no particular reason) is used with *ki-ga suru*
as in

> *Nan-to-naku, kyoo kuru yoona ki-ga shimasu.*

Since this expression implies that the speaker does not have any particularly sound reason, it is used when expressing one's opinion in a reserved
way. For instance, when politely criticizing someone's plan, you might say

> *Amari yaku-ni tatanai yoona ki-ga shimasu.*
> (I have a feeling it won't be very useful.)

or

> *Doomo amari yoku nai yoona ki-ga shimasu.*
> (I have a feeling it isn't so good.)

And *ki-ga suru* is used when agreeing with someone, as in

> *Ee, sonna ki-ga shimasu-ne.*
> (Yes, I feel that way, too.)

(July 6, 1980)

　　　きょう来ると思います

と言うと、その人が来ると信じるだけの理由があるという印象を与えるが、

　　　きょう来るような気がします

と言うと、来ると考えるだけのはっきりした理由は何もないという感じがする。
「気がする」の前には「なんとなく」が使われることが多い。

　　　なんとなく、きょう来るような気がします

　この表現は、そう思うだけの特にしっかりした理由はないという意味合いをも
つので、控えめに意見を表明するのに用いられる。たとえば、だれかの計画を礼
儀に外れぬよう批判するには、

　　　あまり役に立たないような気がします

とか、

　　　どうもあまりよくないような気がします

のような表現が用いられる。また賛意を示す時に、

　　　ええ、そんな気がしますね

のようにも用いられる。

（1980.7.6）

# *'Kono'-to 'Sono'*
## 「この」と「その」
### 'This' and 'that'

Mr. Lerner went to the barber yesterday evening. While waiting his turn, he listened to the conversation between the barber and his customer. The customer said, looking at his hair in the mirror,

*Soko-wa moo sukoshi mijikaku.*
(Make that place a little shorter, please.)

Then the barber said

*A, koko-desu-ne. Kono-kurai-desu-ka.*
(This part? About this much?)

and the customer answered

*Un, sono kurai.*
(Yes, about that much.)

Mr. Lerner was interested in the use of *koko* and *kono*, and of *soko* and *sono*. The customer used *soko* and *sono* although he was referring to his own hair, and the barber said *koko* and *kono* when referring to somebody else's hair.

*       *       *

The difference between *kono* and *sono* (or, between *koko* and *soko*) is that *kono* is used to refer to what is close to the speaker and *sono* is used to refer to what is close to the listener. Thus, one usually says

# 「この」と「その」

## 'This' and 'that'

　きのうの夕方、Mr. Lerner は理髪店に行った。順番を待つ間、理容師と客の会話を聞いていると、客が鏡にうつった自分の髪を見ながら、

　　　そこはもう少し短く

と言った。

　すると理容師は、

　　　あ、ここですね、このくらいですか

と言い、客は、

　　　うん、そのくらい

と答えた。

　この「ここ」「この」と「そこ」「その」の使いかたに、Mr. Lerner は興味をもった。客は自分自身の髪のことを言っているのに「そこ」「その」を用い、理容師はほかの人の髪をさして「ここ」「この」と言っているのである……。

　　　　　　＊　　　　　　＊　　　　　　＊

　「この」と「その」（あるいは「ここ」と「そこ」）の違いは、「この」は話し手に近いものについて言い、「その」は聞き手に近いものをさして言う。したがって普通は、人に何か渡す時は、

*Kore, doozo.*

(Please take this.)

when handing something to someone. And you will ask someone

*Sumimasen. Soko-no hon, totte-kudasaimasen-ka.*

(I'm sorry to trouble you, but could you please hand me the book there?)

The distinction of whether something is close to the speaker or to the listener is not just a matter of physical distance but also of the relationship to the person. Therefore, when the barber was cutting the customer's hair, the hair was closely related to the barber, and even the owner of the hair, namely the customer, regarded it as belonging to the barber at the moment. Thus the customer used *sono* and the barber used *kono*.

In the same way, when you ask someone to give a message to another person, you should say

*Koo tsutaete-kudasaimasen-ka.*

(Will you tell him this?)

before stating the message, and

*Soo tsutaete-kudasaimasen-ka.*

after stating it. The idea is that the message belongs to you before you pass it on, and afterward it belongs to the listener.

When reporting someone's statement, one usually says

*Tanaka-san-ga soo iimashita.*

(Mr. Tanaka said so.)

However, you can also say

　　　これ、どうぞ

と言い、相手のそばのものをさして、

　　　すみません。そこの本、取ってくださいませんか

と言う。

　　あるものが話し手に近いか聞き手に近いかは、物理的な距離の問題に限らず、人との関係によっても決まる。理容師が客の髪を刈っていた場合、客の髪は理容師に近かったから、髪の持ち主つまり客は、その瞬間、自分の髪を理容師に近いものと見なして「その」を使い、理容師は「この」を使ったのである。

　　同じように、だれかに伝言を頼む場合、伝言の内容を言う前には

　　　こう伝えてくださいませんか

と言い、伝言の内容を言い終わったあとは、

　　　そう伝えてくださいませんか

と言う。それは、相手に言う前の伝言は自分に属し、言ってしまったあとは相手に属するからである。

　　人の発言を伝える時は、

　　　田中さんがそう言いました

と言うが、

　　　田中さんはこう言いました

と言う場合もある。それはその発言になお関心を抱きつづけ、まだ相手に伝え切っていないと感じる場合である。

（1982.10.31）

*Tanaka-san-ga koo iimashita.*

(Mr. Tanaka said this.)

when you feel that you are still concerned with the statement and have not yet completely handed the matter over to the listener.

(October 31, 1982)

# *Ippai nomu*
## いっぱい のむ
### To have a drink

Mr. Lerner and Mr. Takada were going out together to visit someone yesterday afternoon, and as Mr. Lerner was getting ready to leave the office Miss Yoshida came to him and asked if he would like a cup of coffee. Mr. Lerner wanted to have some, so he called out to Mr. Takada, who was talking with someone in another corner of the room. Mr. Lerner said in a loud voice

*Ippai nonde-kara ikimashoo.*

(lit., Let's go out after we've had a cup.)

Before Mr. Takada could answer, everyone in the room looked at Mr. Lerner and Miss Yoshida laughed.

*　　　　*　　　　*

# いっぱい飲む

## *To have a drink*

　昨日の午後、Mr. Lerner と Mr. Okada は人を訪ねるため、会社をいっしょに出ることになった。Mr. Lerner が出る準備をしているところへ Miss Yoshida が来て、コーヒーを飲まないかと言った。Mr. Lerner は飲んでから行きたいと思ったので、Mr. Takada にも声をかけようと思った。Mr. Takada は部屋の反対側のすみでだれかと話していたので、こちらから声をはりあげて、

　　　イッパイ飲ンデカラ行キマショウ

とどなった。Mr. Takada は何か言おうとしたが、それより早く部屋にいた人たちがいっせいに Mr. Lerner のほうを見た。Miss Yoshida はおかしそうに笑った……。

To count liquids in a cup or glass, one uses such counter words as *ippai* (one cup), *nihai* (two cups), *sanbai* (three cups), etc.; *hai* or *pai* or *bai* stands for a cup or glass. These counter words are used as in

*Ocha-o sanbai nomimashita.*
(I had three cups of tea.)
*Koohii-o ippai nomimashoo.*
(Let's have a cup of coffee.)

But when one just says *ippai nomimashita* without specifying what one drank, it usually means that the speaker had some alcoholic beverage. Thus Mr. Takada thought that Mr. Lerner was going with him after having some beer or sake or other alcoholic beverage. If someone invites you, saying

*Ippai nomi-ni ikimashoo-ka.*

it means that he wants to have some alcoholic beverage with you.

In this usage, *ippai* does not necessarily mean just one glass; *ippai* actually stands for "some" or "little."

There are other words with "one" meaning "some." *Hito-yasumi* which literally means "one rest" actually means "resting awhile" as in

*Kono hen-de hito-yasumi shimasen-ka.*
(Shall we take a rest now?)

Several other expressions with *hito-* are often used in daily conversation. *Hito-nemuri* (sleeping awhile), *hito-shigoto* (a unit of work) and *hito-furo* (a bath) are a few examples.

The word *hitotsu* (one) is often used for proposing or offering something as in

　茶碗やコップに入った液体を数える時は、1杯、2杯、3杯と数える。「はい」「ぱい」「ばい」は茶碗やコップの意味である。この助数詞は、

　　　お茶を3杯飲みました
　　　コーヒーを1杯飲みましょう

のように用いる。

　しかし、何を飲んだかを言わずただ「1杯飲みました」と言う場合は、通常アルコール飲料を飲んだことを意味する。このため、Mr. Lerner の言ったことは、酒かビールなどのアルコール類を飲んでから行く、という意味にとられたのである。もしだれかが、

　　　1杯飲みに行きましょうか

と言ったなら、それはいっしょに酒を飲もうと誘っているのである。

　この用法では、1杯と言っても必ずしもコップに1杯とは限らない。「1杯」は「いくらか」あるいは「少し」の意味で用いられている。

　「ひとつ」の意味が「少し」になる例は他にもある。「ひと休み」は文字通りには「ひとつ休むこと」だが、実際には「少しの間休むこと」であって、

　　　このへんでひと休みしませんか

のように用いる。

　ほかにも「ひと」がついた表現はいくつか日常会話で用いられる。「ひと眠り」「ひと仕事」「ひとふろ」などはその例である。

　「ひとつ」は提案したり物をすすめたりする時によく用いられる。

　　　ひとついかがですか
　　　ひとつためしてください

*Hitotsu ikaga-desu-ka.*

(Won't you have some?)

*Hitotsu tameshite-kudasai.*

(Please try it.)

Saying *hitotsu ikaga-desu-ka* doesn't necessarily mean that the speaker wants you to have just one; you can go ahead and have several.

(June 8, 1980)

# *Naorimashita*
## なおりました
### It has been repaired

Mr. Lerner took his cassette tape recorder to an electric appliance store the other day to have it fixed. He went back to the store today and asked for it, saying

*Naoshimashita-ka.*

(Have you repaired it?)

Then the clerk said, while bringing his recorder

*Hai, naorimashita.*

(Yes, it has been repaired.)

Mr. Lerner wondered if *Naoshimashita* was wrong. He remembered that when he had said *Kaze-o naoshimashita* (lit., I cured my cold) a few days before, Miss Yoshida had corrected it to *Kaze-ga naorimashita* (lit., My cold has been cured.)

のようにである。「ひとついかが」というのは、必ずしもほんのひとつだけ食べてほしいという意味ではない。遠慮なく３つ４つ食べてもさしつかえない。

(1980.6.8)

# なおりました

## It has been repaired

このあいだ Mr. Lerner は電気器具店へカセットレコーダーを持って行って、修理を頼んだ。きょうその店へ取りに行って、

　　ナオシマシタカ

とたずねると、店員はレコーダーを持ち出してきて、

　　はい、なおりました

と言った。

「ナオシマシタ」ではいけないのだろうか。数日前「カゼヲナオシマシタ」と言った時も、Miss Yoshida に「かぜがなおりました」となおされたことを Mr. Lerner は思い出した……。

*　　　　*　　　　*

When referring to curing some sickness, the word *naoru* (to be recovered) is usually used rather than *naosu* (to cure) whether or not one has tried to cure it. *Naosu* is used only when one wants to emphasize one's own strong will to cure a sickness, as in

*Byooki-o naosu koto-ga ichiban taisetsu-desu.*

(The most important thing is to try to cure your illness.)

Since *naosu* implies a strong will or effort, the clerk at the electric appliance store avoided using it; if he had said

*Hai, naoshimashita.*

that would have sounded boastful and inappropriate.

When one refers to a service he has performed for the listener, it is polite to describe the action as if it has been done without special effort. For instance, when serving tea, it sounds more modest to say

*Ocha-ga hairimashita.*

(Tea is ready —lit., Tea has been poured.)

than

*Ocha-o iremashita.*

(I made tea.)

Sometimes the Japanese choose completely different expressions to avoid using a verb that directly describes their actions. For instance, when someone has written a letter of recommendation, he may say

*Moo dekite-imasu-yo.*

(It's ready now.)

(March 14, 1982)

　　　　　　＊　　　　　　＊　　　　　　＊

　病気の治癒については、なおそうと努力したか否かに関係なく、「なおす」ではなく「なおる」が普通は用いられる。「なおす」は、病気を治療しようという強い意志を強調する時にのみ用いられる。たとえば、

　　　病気をなおすことが一番大切です

のように言う。
　「なおす」は強い意志や努力を意味するから、電気器具店の店員はそれを使わなかった。もし、

　　　はい、なおしました

と言ったら、自慢しているようでおかしいからである。
　相手のために何かしたということを言うには、その行為が特別の努力を伴わずに行われたように言うのが礼儀である。たとえばお茶を出す時、

　　　お茶が入りました

と言うほうが、

　　　お茶を入れました

より謙虚な印象を与える。
　時には、実際にとった行動をそのまま描写するのを避けて、全く別の表現を選ぶこともある。たとえば推薦状を書いた時、

　　　もうできていますよ

と言う場合などである。

（1982.3.14）

# *Ocha-demo nomimasen-ka*
## お茶でも のみませんか
### How about having some tea?

A few days ago Mr. Lerner ran into Mr. Okada on the street. Mr. Okada suggested that they go to a coffee shop nearby, saying

*Ocha-demo nomimasen-ka.*

(How about having some tea?)

At the coffee shop, however, he actually ordered coffee instead of tea, and Mr. Lerner learned that *demo* in *ocha-demo* means ". . . or something like that" rather than "even."

Then yesterday afternoon, when Miss Yoshida asked what his sister Margaret was studying in college, he was not sure so he said

*Suugaku-demo benkyoo-shite-imasu.*

meaning "She's studying mathematics or something like that." Miss Yoshida understood but said that *suugaku-demo* somehow sounded strange.

*   *   *

*Demo* meaning ". . . or something like that" is quite often used when suggesting, as in

*Eega-demo mimashoo-ka.*

(How about going to a movie?)

*Satoo-san-demo sasoimashoo.*

(Let's ask Mr. Sato.)

# お茶でも飲みませんか

*How about having some tea?*

　数日前、Mr. Lerner は偶然、道で Mr. Okada に行き会った。Mr. Okada は近くの喫茶店を指さして、

　　お茶でも飲みませんか

と誘った。

　しかし、喫茶店に入ると、実際には紅茶ではなくコーヒーを注文した。「お茶でも」の「でも」は "even" の意味ではなく "something like that" の意味だったのだなと、Mr. Lerner は悟った。

　そこで昨日の午後、Miss Yoshida に、妹の Margaret は大学で何を勉強しているかと聞かれた時、はっきり知らなかったので、

　　数学デモ勉強シテイマス

と言った。「数学か何かそんなもの」というつもりだったのだが、Miss Yoshida は、わかることはわかるけれど変だと言った……。

＊　　　　　＊　　　　　＊

　「でも」は「～かまたはそのようなもの」という意味で、人に提案をする時に暗示的に、

　　映画でも見ましょうか
　　佐藤さんでも誘いましょう

In such situations, *ocha-demo* or *eega-demo* is preferred to *ocha-o* or *eega-o* because it lets the listener choose what he likes among several possibilities. You can order coffee or coke instead of tea at a coffee shop when you have said *ocha-demo* instead of *ocha-o*.

*Demo* is also used when offering advice:

A: *Mada jikan-ga aru-n-desu-kedo.*

(I have some time to kill.)

B: *Ja, shinbun-demo yondara doo-desu-ka.*

(Then why don't you read a newspaper or something?)

But *demo* in this sense cannot be used to state a fact or to refer to what actually happened. Therefore *Suugaku-demo benkyoo-shite-imasu* cannot be accepted. Mr. Lerner should have said, *Suugaku-ka nanika benkyoo-shite-imasu* to mean "She's studying mathematics or something like that." *ka nanika* can be used both in suggesting something and in stating a fact. Thus:

*Hima-dattara shinbun-demo yondara doo-desu-ka. Asoko-ni Japan Taimuzu-ka nanika arimasu-yo.*

(If you have some time to kill, why don't you read a newspaper? There's a Japan Times or something over there.)

(May 29, 1977)

のようによく用いる。このような場合、「お茶でも」「映画でも」というほうが、「お茶を」「映画を」より好まれるのは、相手がいくつかの可能性の中から好きなものを選べるようにするからである。「お茶を」ではなく「お茶でも」と言えば、喫茶店で紅茶の代わりにコーヒーやコーラを注文することができるわけである。

人に助言する時も「でも」が用いられる。

A：まだ時間があるんですけど……
B：じゃ、新聞でも読んだらどうですか

しかし、この意味の「でも」は、事実を述べたり、現実に起こったことに言及する場合には、使うことができない。したがって、「数学デモ勉強シテイマス」は許容されない。Mr. Lerner は「数学か何か勉強しています」と言うべきであった。「〜か何か」なら、暗示にも叙述にも用いることができる。したがってこんな言いかたになる。

ひまだったら、新聞でも読んだらどうですか。あそこにジャパンタイムズか何かありますよ。

▶幅を持たせた例示表現によって、相手に対する遠慮や思いやりを示す例は、「でも」の他、「〜たり」「〜など」など多数見られる。こうした表現の「幅」は、適切に使えば効果的である。「あいまい」として退ける前に表現効果から検討すべきものである。

(1977.5.29)

# Chapter 2

# Difference from English

英語との違い

Not only native speakers of English but also speakers of other languages study Japanese through English, and naturally differences between Japanese and English are an important matter to such people in using Japanese. We often refer to this matter, but in this chapter in particular we discuss how direct translation from English must be avoided.

In English one says "I think I'll read them," but if you translate this into Japanese as *yomu-to omoimasu*, it usually means that someone other than the speaker himself reads them; you must use the volitional form *yomoo* when referring to one's own intentions. Saying "I don't learn it" means you have not acquired the knowledge, but saying *naraimasen* means that you will not study it, since "learn" and *narau* have a different usage. When describing a thin person, you have to say *yaseta hito*, literally someone who has grown thin. *Shirimasen* can mean that you are not involved in the matter, so if you translate "I don't know" directly into Japanese, you are likely to sound indifferent to the matter. Also, *iku* and *kuru* are not the same as "come" and "go."

The expression of desire is particularly important in this respect. In English you can use "want to" or "would like to" with anyone, but *-tai* (I want) can be used only with the speaker himself or someone equal to him. Politeness must be considered in using *-tai*.

英語を母語とする人に限らず、英語を通じて日本語を学ぶ人も多く、英語からの直訳が誤解や笑いを生むことはめずらしくない。本書でも、英語からの直訳では理解できない日本語について各所で触れているが、はっきりと英語との対応が表れている例をいくつかここに集めた。

　「読もうと思います」は、英語では自分の行動についての考えを I think I'll read it. のように言うことができるが、日本語で「読むと思います」と言うと、話し手以外の人が読むと話し手は思う、という意味になる。「読もう」という形で話し手の意志であることを示す必要があることを説明している。「習いません」は英語で I don't learn it.「まだ習熟していない」の意味になるが、日本語の「習わない」は学習しないという意味になり、誤解を招く可能性がある。「やせる人」については序文でも述べたが、やせた状態を言うには「やせた」を使わなければならないのであって、日本語の「た」を過去を表すものとだけきめてはならないことを説いている。「知りません」が単に情報をもたないという意味でなく、他者に対する断絶を示す場合があるので、I don't know. と区別して使わなければならないことを示している。日本語の「行く」と「来る」は英語の go と come の場合と違う用法があることは、英語を学ぶ日本人にも参考になるであろう。

　とくに注意すべきは「日光へ行きたいです」の「〜たい」の用法で、英語では want や would like to が話し手についても聞き手についても言えるが、日本語の「〜たい」は主体が限られるということに、日本語の持つ待遇性の問題があることは重要な問題である。

# *Naraimasen*
## ならいません
### I won't study it

The other day Miss Yoshida asked Mr. Lerner if his name has any special meaning. She was obviously referring to the fact that his last name "Lerner" has the same pronunciation as "learner." Mr. Lerner said that he didn't know and added

*Demo chittomo nihongo-o naraimasen.*

meaning "I can't learn Japanese at all." Miss Yoshida said that was not true because he is studying it very hard. He realized then that *naraimasen* is not an exact equivalent of "don't learn."

\*　　　　　\*　　　　　\*

The Japanese verb *narau* stresses the action of studying or making efforts to acquire knowledge as in

*Ikebana-o naratte-imasu.*
(I am studying flower arrangement.)
*Juudoo-o naraimasen-ka.*
(Why don't you study judo?)

It does not imply the acquisition of knowledge by studying. If you say

*Nihongo-o chittomo naraimasen.*

# 習いません

### I won't study it

　このあいだ Miss Yoshida が Mr. Lerner に、ラーナーさんの名前には特別の意味があるのかとたずねた。"Lerner" の発音が "learner"（学習者）と同じだから、ということであろう。Mr. Lerner はわからないと答え、

　　　デモ、チットモ日本語ヲ習イマセン

と言った。日本語がうまくならないという意味で言ったのであるが、Miss Yoshida は、それは違う、よく勉強しているではないかと言った。それで気がついたのであるが、「ナライマセン」と "don't learn" はどうも同じではないようである……。

＊　　　　＊　　　　＊

　日本語の「習う」は、学習行動あるいは知識獲得の努力を強調するもので、

　　　生け花を習っています
　　　柔道を習いませんか

のように言う。学習によって知識を獲得し終わるという意味ではない。

　　　日本語ヲチットモ習イマセン

と言うと、「日本語が進歩しない」ということではなく、「日本語の学習を始めていない」という意味になる。また、

it will mean that you haven't started learning Japanese, instead of meaning "I don't make any progress in Japanese." And if you say

*Kesshite nihongo-o naraimasen.*

you will sound as if you are determined not to study Japanese for some reason, since *kesshite* indicates the speaker's determination.

To express the fact that you cannot easily learn and become good at something, you should say

*Nakanaka joozu-ni narimasen.*

(lit., I don't easily become good at it.)

or

*Nakanaka oboeraremasen.*

(lit., I can't easily memorize it.)

For a more sophisticated expression, you can say

*Nakanaka mi-ni tsukimasen.*

or

*Nakanaka mono-ni narimasen.*

It may help to memorize the sentence

*Naratte-imasu-ga oboeraremasen.*

(I'm studying it but I can't learn it.)

(October 14, 1981)

ケッシテ日本語ヲ習イマセン

と言うと、何らかの理由があって、絶対に日本語を学習するまいと決心している
ように聞こえる。「けっして」は話し手の決意を示すからである。
　学習が容易に進まない、上達しないという事実を述べるには、

　　　なかなか上手になりません

とか、

　　　なかなかおぼえられません

と言ったほうがよい。
　さらに進んだ表現としては、

　　　なかなか身につきません

とか、

　　　なかなかものになりません

と言ってもよい。

　　　習ってはいますが、おぼえられません

という文を暗記しておくと役に立つかもしれない。

（1981.10.4）

# *Yaseru hito?*
# やせる人
### A person who is getting thinner?

While several people were leisurely talking during their coffee break, Mr. Lerner mentioned that he drinks beer every day. Mr. Takada asked him when he drinks it, and Mr. Lerner answered that he drinks it when he returns home. He used the phrase,

*Uchi-e kaeru toki.*

(When I return home.)

Then Mr. Takada asked where he drinks. Mr. Lerner was puzzled but replied that of course it was at home. This time Mr. Takada looked puzzled, and seemed to want further explanation, but the coffee break was over so the discussion had to be stopped.

&ast; &ast; &ast;

To say that you like to have a glass of beer "when you return home," you have to say *uchi-e kaetta toki*, instead of saying *uchi-e kaeru toki*. (*Kaetta* is the past tense of *kaeru*.) Since the verb *kaeru* actually refers to the process of going home rather than reaching home, *uchi-e kaeru toki* means "when you are on your way home." That is why Mr. Takada was curious to know at what bar Mr. Lerner was drinking.

*Kaetta toki* actually means "when you have completed the action of going home," so you can say

*Uchi-e kaetta toki biiru-o nomimasu.*

# やせる人?

### *A person who is getting thinner?*

　会社のコーヒー・ブレイクの時間の雑談中、Mr. Lerner が毎日ビールを飲むと言うと、Mr. Takada がいつ飲むのかとたずねた。家へ帰った時飲むというつもりで、

　　　ウチへ帰ルトキ

と言うと、Mr. Takada は重ねて、「どこで」とたずねる。Mr. Lerner は変だとは思ったが「モチロン家デ」と答えた。今度は Mr. Takada のほうが変な顔をして、説明を求める様子を見せたが、ちょうど休み時間が終わり、話はそれきりになってしまった……。

　　　　　　*　　　　　　　*　　　　　　　*

　ビールを飲むのが "when you return home" であるなら、「家へ帰る時」ではなく「家へ帰った時」と言わなければならない。「帰る」という動詞は、実際には帰りつくことを言うのではなく、家へ帰って行く過程を示すのであるから、「家へ帰る時」と言うと、「帰宅の途中」という意味になる。それで Mr. Takada は Mr. Lerner がどこのバーで飲むかをたずねたのである。

　「帰った時」は「帰るという行為を完了した時」の意味であるから、帰宅後飲むなら、

　　　家へ帰った時ビールを飲みます

と言う。

to mean that you drink beer when you are at home.

To express that some action has been completed, you have to use verbs in the past tense. *Kekkon-suru hito* means a person who is going to get married, while *kekkon-shita hito* refers to someone who has already gotten married.

Similarly the past tense of the verb *yaseru*, "to become thin," is used in modifying a person, *yaseta hito*. If you say *yaseru hito*, it gives the unlikely picture of a person who is getting thinner and thinner before your very eyes.

*Kaetta*, *kekkon-shita*, *yaseta*, these can be called the past forms, but the Japanese idea of the past is quite different from that of English-speakers.

(October 31, 1976)

# *Kaette-kudasai*
## かえってください
### Please go home

Last Saturday Mr. Takada came to visit Mr. Lerner. The two had a very good time together, and when Mr. Takada left, Mr. Lerner really wished to have him come again, so he said,

　ある行為が完了したことを表すには、過去形の動詞を用いなければならない。「結婚する人」と言うと、これから結婚する人で、「結婚した人」はすでに結婚している人である。

　同様に、「やせる」も、人の姿を形容する時には「やせた」人としなければならない。「やせる人」と言うと、目の前でだんだんやせていく人のような印象を与えるので、現実性が薄い。

　「帰った」「結婚した」「やせた」などを「過去形」とは言うが、日本語の過去形は英語のそれとは全く異なるのである。

> ▶助動詞「た」には
> ①過去の事実を表す、②完了の事実を表す、③その他、確認・回想・命令などを表す、の用法があり、テンスだけでなくアスペクトの面からも考察しなければならない。便宜上 past tense という語を用いることが多いが、実際にはここに述べたような②の用法に注意しなければならない。

(1976.10.31)

# 帰ってください

*Please go home*

　先週の土曜日、Mr. Lerner のところへ Mr. Takada が訪ねてきた。楽しく語り合って Mr. Takada が帰ろうとした時、Mr. Lerner はぜひまた近いうちに来てほしいと思ったので、

*Sugu kaette-kudasai.*

meaning "Please come back soon."

Mr. Takada looked astonished, remained silent for a while, and then burst out laughing. He knew English well enough to understand why this mistake happened; to come back means to come again, and Mr. Lerner directly translated "come back" as *kaeru.*

When Mr. Takada explained that *Kaette-kudasai* means "Please go home," Mr. Lerner could not laugh. He was afraid that he had made the same mistake before.

*       *       *

The verb *kaeru* does not mean "to come back to the place where one is now." It means "to go back to the place where one belongs." Usually one's home is where one belongs; therefore, *kaerimasu* means "I'm going home" and *Kaette-kudasai* means "Please go home." If you want your visitor to come again, you have to say,

*Mata kite-kudasai.*
(Please come again.)

Places other than one's home can be where one belongs, too. One's job can be where one belongs, depending on how one feels about it. Also, in the case of inhabitants in big cities who are from the country, they often feel their hometown is where they belong. So they say *kuni-e kaerimasu* when they visit their parents in the country.

A friend's house or a store is not usually where you belong. When you are visiting someone for a few hours, or buying things at a store and leave for a short while, you should say *modotte-kimasu.* If you say to a storekeeper *kaerimasu* when you intend to come back after getting some money

　　　スグ帰ッテクダサイ

と言った。

　Mr. Takada はびっくりした顔をして一瞬おし黙ったが、やがてぷっと吹き出した。英語のできる Mr. Takada には、この間違いの原因がわかったのだ。come back には「また来る」の意味があるが、Mr. Lerner はこの come back を「帰る」と直訳してしまったのである。

　Mr. Takada が、「帰ッテクダサイ」は "Please go home." の意味であると説明すると、Mr. Lerner の顔はこわばった。もしかすると同じ間違いを前にもしたかもしれないのだ……。

　　　　　　　＊　　　　　　　＊　　　　　　　＊

　「帰る」という動詞は「今いるところへ戻ってくる」ことを意味するのではない。「本来いるべきところへ戻る」の意味である。通常自宅は本来いるべき場所であるから、「帰ります」といえば「家へ帰る」ことになり、「帰ってください」は「自宅へ戻ってください」の意味になる。訪問者の再訪を望むなら、

　　　また来てください

と言わなければならない。

　自宅のほかにも、その人のいるべきところだと考えられる場所はある。職場も、その人の感じかたによっては、本来いるべき所となる。また、田舎から出てきて大都市に住んでいる人は、故郷を本来いるべきところだと感じ、田舎に住む両親を訪ねる時、「国へ帰ります」と言う人も多い。

　友人の家とか商店などは、通常人の本来いるべき場所ではない。だれかのところに数時間滞在している時や買い物をしている時に、一時的にその場所を離れる場合には、「戻ってきます」と言う。店で買い物中に、銀行から金を出したり電話をかけたりするために一度外に出る時、「帰ります」と言うと、店員のほうは、

at the bank or after making a telephone call, he may think you gave up and went home and end up selling what you want to buy. You can ask him to save something for you by saying,

*Sugu modotte-kimasu-kara totte-oite-kudasai.*

(I'll be back soon, so please save this for me.)

(November 14, 1976)

# *Shirimasen*
## 知りません
*I don't know*

During the coffee break a few days ago Miss Yoshida asked Mr. Lerner if he had any plans for the next Saturday. Since he did not know yet, Mr. Lerner answered

*Shirimasen.*

(I don't know.)

Miss Yoshida looked confused and asked Mr. Takada to help her. She said that she wanted to invite Mr. Lerner as well as Mr. Takada and a few others to a party at her home, but that she did not dare ask him because she didn't understand his answer.

What was wrong with saying *Shirimasen* for "I don't know"?

       \*             \*             \*

In the situation mentioned above, a Japanese would say

買うのをやめて家へ帰るのだと思って、その人が買おうと思っていた物を人に売ってしまうかもしれない。その品物を取っておいてもらいたいと思ったら、

　　すぐ戻ってきますから、取っておいてください

と頼むことである。

(1976.11.14)

# 知りません

### *I don't know*

　2、3日前のコーヒー・ブレイクの時、Miss Yoshida が Mr. Lerner に、次の土曜日の予定は決まっているかとたずねた。予定は決まっていなかったので、

　　知リマセン

と答えると、Miss Yoshida は困った顔をして、Mr. Takada に助けを求めた。彼女の言うには、Mr. Lerner、Mr. Takada、その他2、3人を家に招いてパーティーをしたいのだが、Mr. Lerner の返事の真意がわからないので、招こうかどうか迷っているということであった。

　「知リマセン」はまずかったのだろうか……。

＊　　　　　＊　　　　　＊

　上のような場面では、「知りません」ではなく、

*Wakarimasen.*

(lit., I don't understand.)

instead of *Shirimasen.* In fact, Japanese say *Wakarimasen* when English-speaking people would say "I don't know." When asked for directions or the time, Japanese often say *Wakarimasen* instead of *Shirimasen.*

*Shirimasen* means that "I haven't had the chance to get the information"; therefore it should be all right to say *Shirimasen* when you do not have the particular knowledge. But in actual usage Japanese prefer saying *Wakarimasen* when they think they should know the answer. Because one should know about oneself better than anything else, to say *Shirimasen* when asked what one is going to do in the future sounds very strange. It can be taken as a blunt statement meaning "It has nothing to do with me," as is actually used when one is angry. When an angry mother says *Shirimasen!* to her naughty child, it means she refuses to have anything to do with him for the time being.

*Wakarimasen* is preferred even when answering a question which does not directly concern oneself because it implies that the lack of knowledge is one's own fault. For example when a student cannot answer the instructor's question, he usually says *Wakarimasen.* It is more polite to say that he does not have the ability to find out than to say that he has not had the chance to learn; insisting on the latter may sound as if he is blaming his instructors for their negligence or is blaming the questioner for asking something he has not learned.

However, when the question is about something one is not expected to know, such as whether one knows a certain person or a place, it is all right to say *Shirimasen.* And also, when the question takes the form . . .-*o shitte-imasu-ka* or more politely, . . .-*o gozonji-desu-ka* (Do you know . . . ?), the answer should be either *Hai, shitte-imasu,* or *Iie, shirimasen.*

(January 16, 1977)

### わかりません

が普通である。英語で "I don't know." と言う時に日本人は「わかりません」と言うことが多い。道順や時刻をたずねられると、「知りません」より「わかりません」をよく使う。

「知りません」は「まだ情報を得ていない」という意味である。したがって何かについての知識を持たない時は、「知りません」と言ってもいいはずである。しかし、実際には、自分は答えを知っているべきだと思う時には、「わかりません」と言う。自分自身についてはだれよりもよく知っているはずであるから、これから何をするかと聞かれて「知りません」と答えるのは、非常に異様にひびく。「わたしの知ったことではない」という不愛想な返事ととられやすいし、実際怒っている時にはそう答える。言うことを聞かない子供に腹を立てた母親が「知りません！」と言うのは、一時子供との関係を絶つことを宣言しているに等しい。

自分自身に直接関係のない質問に対しても、「わかりません」のほうが好まれるのは、知識の欠如は自分の責任ととる態度を示すからである。たとえば学生が教師の質問に答えられない時、「わかりません」が普通である。答える能力がないと言うほうが、学習する機会がなかったと言うより礼儀正しい。機会がなかったと主張することは、教師の教育上の怠慢や、学習していないことを聞く不手際を責めているようにひびく恐れがある。

しかし、質問の内容が単にだれかを知っているか、ある場所を知っているかというようなことで、知っていなければならないという性質のものでなければ、「知りません」でよい。

また、質問は「〜を知っていますか」あるいはもっと丁寧な場合には「〜をご存じですか」という形をとるが、答えは「はい、知っています」あるいは「いいえ、知りません」となる。

(1977.1.16)

# *Nikkoo-e ikitai-desu*
## 日光へ いきたいです
### I want to go to Nikko

Mr. Lerner's sister Margaret wrote that she was coming to Japan next month. Mr. Takada and Miss Yoshida, his co-workers, started discussing which of various famous spots he should take her to first. Mr. Lerner recalled what Margaret had said in her letter and said,

*Nikkoo-e ikitai-desu.*

meaning "she wants to go to Nikko."

But Miss Yoshida said, *Ara, Raanaa-san-mo?* (Oh, you too, Mr. Lerner?), obviously taking his comment as "I want to go to Nikko." Mr. Lerner had been told by his Japanese teacher that one does not have to mention the subject of the sentence unless it has to be emphasized. Did he have to start his sentence with *imooto-wa . . .* (my sister . . .)?

*     *     *

Miss Yoshida would not have misunderstood Mr. Lerner if he had said

*Nikkoo-e ikitagatte-imasu.*

(She wants to go to Nikko.)

instead of saying *Nikkoo-e ikitai-desu.* Words ending in *-tai* are used to indicate the speaker's wishes while those ending in *-tagaru* are used to show the wishes of someone else. Thus *ikitai-desu* usually means "I want to go," and *ikitagatte-imasu* means "*he* wants to go," "*she* wants to go," or "*they* want to go."

# 日光へ行きたいです

*I want to go to Nikko*

Mr. Lerner の妹 Margaret が来月日本へ来るというたよりがあった。同僚の Mr. Takada と Miss Okada は、Mr. Lerner がまずどこへ彼女を案内すべきか、議論を始めた。Mr. Lerner は Margaret が手紙の中で言っていたことを思い出して、

　　　日光へ行キタイデス

と言った。もちろん、Margaret の希望を伝えるつもりだった。

　ところが Miss Yoshida は「あら、ラーナーさんも？」と言った。どうやら彼の言ったことを "I want to go to Nikko." の意味にとったらしい。Mr. Lerner は、日本語の先生が、強調の必要がない時は主語を言う必要がない、と言ったのを守ったのだ。「妹は……」と言うべきだったのだろうか……。

　　　*　　　　　　*　　　　　　*

Mr. Lerner がもし「日光へ行キタイデス」と言わず、

　　　日光へ行きたがっています

と言ったのだったら、Miss Yoshida は誤解しなかったであろう。「たい」で終わる語は話し手の願望を表し、「たがる」に終わる語はだれか他の人の願望を表す。したがって「行きたいです」は通常 "I want to go"「行きたがっています」は "*he* wants to go" "*she* wants to go" あるいは "*they* want to go" の意味になる。

In a similar way, certain expressions that are used to express the speaker's feelings cannot be used for third persons. For instance, *Ureshii-desu* or *Kanashiidesu* means "I'm happy." or "I'm unhappy." It is not appropriate to say *Yoshida-san-wa ureshii-desu* (Miss Yoshida is happy) or *Imooto-wa kanashii-desu* (My sister is unhappy). When referring to others, you have to change the last part of the words:

*Yoshida-san-wa ureshisoo-desu.*
(Miss Yoshida looks happy.)
*Imooto-wa kanashisoo-desu.*
(My sister looks unhappy.)

The idea behind this distinction is that one cannot know another's feelings with certainty but can only judge by his appearance. In other words, you cannot say that someone is happy in Japanese; you must say he *looks* happy.

Returning to the distinction between *ikitai* and *ikitagaru*, the same logic can be seen; only the speaker himself knows what he wants to do, and in referring to others one has to use *-tagaru* which means "to act like wanting to do something."

This distinction between expressions referring to the speaker himself and those referring to others is one of the devices that makes it possible to often omit the subject of the sentence in Japanese.

(May 1, 1977)

　同様に、話し手の感情を表すいくつかの語は、三人称に用いることができない。「嬉しいです」「悲しいです」は "I'm happy" "I'm unhappy" の意味である。「吉田サンハウレシイデス」とか「妹ハ悲シイデス」と言うのは不適切である。他者については語尾を変えて、

　　　吉田さんは嬉しそうです
　　　妹は悲しそうです

としなければならない。

　こうした区別の背後には、他の人の感情を正確に知ることは不可能で、外観から判断するほかはない、という考えがある。言いかえれば、日本語では "someone is happy" とは言えず、"someone *looks* happy" と言わなければならないのである。

　「行きたい」と「行きたがる」の区別についても、同じことが言える。話し手自身でなければ自分の欲求は知り得ないし、他の人について話す時は「〜したいように行動する」という意味の「たがる」をつけなければならない。

　話者自身に関する表現と他者に関する表現の区別も、日本語の文の主語がしばしば省かれることを可能にする役を果たしている。

　▶話者自身の欲求に関しても、自己を客観化した時は、「子供の時はよく甘い物を食べたがったものだ」のように、「たがる」を用いる。過去の自己をいわば三人称として扱っているからである。

（1977.5.1）

# *Arigatoo-gozaimashita*
## ありがとうございました
### Thank you for having been so kind

A few weeks ago Mr. Lerner was asked to give a short speech at a gathering of several dozen businessmen, and talked about his experiences in Japan. When his speech came to an end, he said with a bow

*Doomo arigatoo-gozaimasu.*

(Thank you very much.)

to thank the audience for listening to his inadequate Japanese.

The audience remained silent for a moment as if they expected him to say something else before they clapped their hands in applause.

Later, Mr. Takada said that Mr. Lerner should have said

*Arigatoo-gozaimashita.*

instead of *Arigatoo-gozaimasu.* After that Mr. Lerner noticed that the Japanese sometimes use this expression *Arigatoo-gozaimashita* in place of *Arigatoo-gozaimasu,* but he didn't understand the difference between the two.

\*　　　　　\*　　　　　\*

When giving factual information, whether one should use the present tense or the past is decided by the facts themselves; you have to say *Kinoo ame-ga furimashita* to mean "It rained yesterday and *Kotoshi sanjuu-desu* to mean "I am now 30 years old." But when expressing feelings, one chooses the tense depending on how one feels. To thank someone, one can use either the present or the past. If one feels that he is grateful now for the

# ありがとうございました

*Thank you for having been so kind*

3週間ほど前、Mr. Lerner は数十人のサラリーマンの集会で、簡単なスピーチをするように依頼され、日本での経験について話した。話が終わった時、つたない日本語を傾聴してくれた聴衆に感謝すべく、おじぎをしながら、

　　　ドウモアリガトウゴザイマス

と言った。聴衆は、まだ彼が何か言うのを期待するかのように一瞬沈黙していたが、やがて拍手が起こった。

あとで Mr. Takada にきいてみると、「アリガトウゴザイマス」でなく、

　　　ありがとうございました

と言うべきだったのだ、ということだった。その後、「ありがとうございます」の代わりに「ありがとうございました」がときどき使われているのに気がついたが、この2つがどう違うのか、Mr. Lerner にはよくわからなかった……。

＊　　　　　＊　　　　　＊

事実をそのまま伝える時に、現在形を使うか過去形を使うかは、事実そのものによって決定する。昨日のことなら「雨が降りました」と言わなければならないし、今年30歳なら、「いま30歳です」と言う。しかし、感情を表す時には、自分の感じかたで時制を選ぶ。人に感謝する時は現在形でも過去形でもよい。親切にしてもらったことに対して、現在感謝しているのなら、「ありがとうございま

favor that someone has done him, he says *Arigatoo-gozaimasu*. If he feels that he should emphasize that the favor has been completed after the passage of some time, he says *Arigatoo-gozaimashita* to mean "Thank you for having been so kind."

The form ending in *-ta* as in *furimashita* or *gozaimashita* is different in its usage from the English verbs in their past forms. Japanese verbs ending in *-ta* (or, sometimes in *-da*) are used to indicate that an action has been completed regardless of whether it took place in the past, takes place in the present, or even in the future. One says

*Ashita okita toki-ni denwa-shimasu.*

(lit., I will call you when I have woken up tomorrow.)

Because *Arigatoo-gozaimashita* signifies that the favor has been completed after the lapse of some time it is appropriate for the speaker to use it when he has completed his speech. Similarly, when one leaves someone after a long time, he often says

*Nagai aida arigatoo-gozaimashita.*

(lit., Thank you for having been kind to me for a long time.)

(December 3, 1978)

# *Yomoo-to omoimasu*
## よもうと おもいます
### I think I'll read them

A few days ago Mr. Lerner decided to take home some of the papers he could not finish reading during the day, and was putting them together

す」と言う。その好意がある程度の時間をかけて行われたということを強調すべきだと思ったら、「ありがとうございました」と言う。英語にすれば "Thank you for having been so kind." となろう。

「降りました」や「ございました」のように「た」に終わる形は、その用法において、英語の過去形動詞とは異なっている。日本語動詞の「た」形（「だ」に終わることもある）は、ある動作が完了したことを示すもので、過去の動作でも現在の動作でも、時には未来のことでもかまわず用いる。

　　　あした起きた時に電話します

とも言うのである。

「ありがとうございました」は、その好意が達成されるのにある程度の時間がかかったことを示すものであるから、スピーチの終わりに用いるのに適切である。同様に長期間一緒にいた人と別れる時はよく、

　　　長い間ありがとうございました

と言う。

（1978.12.3）

# 読もうと思います

### I think I'll read them

　2、3日前のこと、Mr. Lerner が昼間読み終われなかった書類を、家へ持って帰ろうと思ってまとめているところへ、Mr. Takada が、もう帰る用意ができて

when Mr. Takada came to see if he was ready to leave. So Mr. Lerner said, pointing to the papers,

*Konban yomu-to omoimasu.*

meaning "I think I'll read them tonight."

But Mr. Takada did not understand and asked *Dare-ga?* (Who's going to?) Mr. Lerner wondered why he asked this; several people had told him that one does not have to mention the subject of the sentence in Japanese when it can be understood from the context.

\*        \*        \*

If Mr. Lerner had said

*Konban yomoo-to omoimasu.*

instead of *Konban yomu-to omoimasu,* Mr. Takada would have immediately understood.

Saying *Yomu-to omoimasu* means that the speaker thinks someone else will read them, instead of the speaker reading them himself.

To indicate the speaker's own intention, a different form of the verb must be used before . . . *to omoimasu* (I think . . .). This form is usually called the volitional; *yomoo* is the volitional form of *yomu,* and *ikoo* (I'll go) is that of *iku* (to go).

Japanese leave out the subject of the sentence whenever they can, but there are certain devices or rules to avoid confusion or misunderstanding. The use of the various verb forms is one of those devices. *Yomoo-to omoimasu* and *Yomu-to omoimasu* are as completely different sentences as "I think I'll read them" and "I think he'll read them" in English.

If asked what you will do tomorrow and you answer

いるか見に来た。そこで Mr. Lerner は書類を指さして、

　　　今晩読ムト思イマス

と言った。

　しかし Mr. Takada は理解せず、「だれが？」と聞く。なぜそんなことを聞くのか。日本語では文脈からわかる主語は、言わなくていいのだと何人もの人が教えたではないか……。

*　　　　　*　　　　　*

　Mr. Lerner が「今晩読ムト思イマス」ではなく、

　　　今晩読もうと思います

と言えば、Mr. Takada は直ちに理解したであろう。

　「読むと思います」というのは、話し手が読むのではなく、だれかほかの人が読むと話し手が思う、という意味になる。

　話し手自身の意図を示すには、「～と思います」の前に、別の動詞の形を使わなければならない。この形は意志形と呼ばれる。「読む」の意志形は「読もう」で、「行く」の意志形は「行こう」である。

　日本語では文の主語は不要の場合省かれるが、それには混乱や誤解を避けるための一定の方法なり規則なりがある。さまざまな動詞の形を用いることも、その方法のひとつである。「読もうと思います」と「読むと思います」は全く別の文である。英語の "I think I'll read them." と "I think he'll read them." が別の文であるのと同じである。

　あした何をするつもりかと聞かれて、

　　　釣リニ行クト思イマス

と答えたら、相手は少々とまどうであろう。前後の状況から考えて、自分のこと

*Tsuri-ni iku-to omoimasu.*

meaning that you intend to go fishing, the listener will be a little puzzled. Although it is clear from the situation that you are referring to yourself, it will still seem strange because it sounds as if you were talking about someone else.

You must be especially careful when you want to add that you don't know for sure yet. If you say

*Tsuri-ni iku-to omoimasu-ga, yoku shirimasen.*

it is even more puzzling because it definitely means that you are talking about someone else. Instead you should say

*Tsuri-ni ikoo-ka-to omoimasu-ga, mada yoku wakarimasen.*
(I think I might go fishing, but I don't know for sure yet.—The *ka* added to *ikoo* shows uncertainty.)

(May 8, 1977)

# *Sore-ni shite-mo*
## それに しても
*Even so*

A few days ago several people including Mr. Lerner were waiting for Mr. Okada to come to the office to discuss some business. Since he didn't

を言っているのだということははっきりしているが、なんだか他人のことを言っているような言いかたなので、異様に聞こえるに違いない。

特に予定がはっきりわからない時には、注意を要する。もし、

　　　釣リニ行クト思イマスガ、ヨク知リマセン

と言ったら、他の人のことを言っていることが一層明確になるので、なお変な印象を与えることになる。

　　　釣りに行こうかと思いますが、まだよくわかりません

と言わなければならない。

(1977.5.8)

# それにしても

*Even so*

数日前、Mr. Lerner ほか何人かの人が、Mr. Okada が商談で訪ねてくるのを待っていた。時刻になっても姿を現さないので雑談を始め、だれかがここ2、3年

show up on time, they started talking. Someone mentioned that he had not been skiing for a few years and they discussed skiing for a while. When that discussion came to an end Mr. Takada looked at his watch and said

*Sore-ni shite-mo Okada-san osoi-desu-ne.*

(Even so, Mr. Okada is late, isn't he?)

Everybody agreed and someone was starting to call him, when Mr. Okada showed up with an apology that the traffic had been very bad.

Mr. Lerner didn't understand the meaning of the phrase *sore-ni shite-mo*, so he later consulted a dictionary. He found several English equivalents such as "even so," "for all that," "still," "nevertheless," "although," and "admitting that." But none of them seemed to fit the sentence Mr. Takada had used. What relation did the discussion of skiing have with Mr. Okada's being late?

*　　　　*　　　　*

*Sore-ni shite-mo* literally means "even though we decide on that"; it is used when expressing one's opinion about something else after admitting what has already been said either by oneself or by another speaker. For instance, suppose two people are wondering why someone is late.

A: *Michi-ga konde-iru-n-deshoo.*

(I guess he is late because the traffic is heavy.)

B: *Sore-ni shite-mo konna-ni okureru hazu-wa nai-deshoo.*

(But he shouldn't be as late as this.)

Here *sore-ni shite-mo* means "admitting what you have said," or "although he may be delayed by the heavy traffic."

This example is easy to understand because we can clearly see what *sore* refers to, but in Mr. Takada's sentence above, *sore-ni shite-mo* seems difficult to understand because *sore* does not refer to what has been said im-

スキーに行っていないと言い出したことから、しばらくスキーの話に花が咲いた。その話が終わると Mr. Takada は時計を見て、

　　　それにしても岡田さんおそいですね

と言った。みんな同感し、だれかが電話しようとしたところへ、交通渋滞にあいましてと言いながら、Mr. Okada が入ってきた。

　Mr. Lerner は「それにしても」という語句の意味がわからなかったので、あとで辞書を引いてみた。英語の訳として "even so," "for all that," "still," "nevertheless," "although," "admitting that" などがあがっていた。しかし、そのいずれも Mr. Takada の使った文には合わない気がした。スキーの話と Mr. Okada の遅れたことと、何の関連があるのだろう……。

　　　　　　　*　　　　　　　*　　　　　　　*

　「それにしても」は文字通りには「そうだと考えても」の意味で、すでに自分自身あるいは他の人の言ったことを認めたあと、何らかの意見を表す時に用いられる。たとえばだれかがまだ来ないのはなぜだろうかと、2人の人が話し合っているとする。

　　　A：道が混んでいるんでしょう
　　　B：それにしても、こんなに遅れるはずはないでしょう

この場合の「それにしても」は「ご意見の正しさは認めても」あるいは「道が混んでいるために遅れるのだとしても」の意味である。

　この場合は「それ」のさすものがはっきりしているので、理解しやすい。しかし上記の Mr. Takada の「それにしても」の場合は、「それ」はすぐ前に言ったことをさしていないので、理解しにくい感じがする。この場合「それ」は、直接に先行するスキーの話そのものをさすのでなく、人々が Mr. Okada を待っているという事実をさしている。この「それにしても」を敷衍すれば、「われわれはス

mediately before. Here, *sore* is used to refer, not to the ski topic which directly precedes it, but to the fact that the people there have been waiting for Mr. Okada. Thus *sore-ni shite-mo* can be paraphrased as "although we have been waiting for him, killing time by discussing things like skiing." *Sore* is usually used to refer to what the speaker or someone else has said, but sometimes it can refer to what has been the topic or the concern of the people engaged in the conversation.

(January 14, 1979)

# *Kyoo ikimasu*
## きょう 行きます
### *I'm coming today*

Yesterday afternoon Mr. Lerner had some business to discuss with Mr. Okada, and was going to call him to ask if it would be all right to visit his office that day. Just then Mr. Okada called, and started asking Mr. Lerner some business questions. Mr. Lerner wanted to answer his question when he visited him, so he said

*Kyoo kuru-to omoimasu.*

meaning "I think I'll come today." Then Mr. Okada asked him *Dare-ga?* (Who is?). Mr. Lerner was surprised and said *Watashi-ga* (I am). Then Mr. Okada quickly said *Aa, kite-kudasaru-n-desu-ka* (Oh, you're coming to see me?).

キーの話などしたりして時間をつぶしながら、彼を待っているのだが」のように
なろう。「それ」は通常話し手かだれかの言ったことをさすが、時には、それま
で話題になったことや、その場の人々の関心事などをさすこともある。

(1979.1.14)

# きょう行きます

## *I'm coming today*

昨日の午後、Mr. Lerner は Mr. Okada と話し合いたいことがあって、会社へ
訪ねていってもいいかどうか聞くために電話しようとした。ちょうどその時、
Mr. Okada から電話が来て、仕事のことで質問をし始めた。Mr. Lerner は会いに
いってから答えたいと思ったので、

　　キョウ来ルト思イマス

と言った。すると Mr. Okada は「だれが？」ときくので、驚いて「わたしが」
と答えた。すると Mr. Okada は「ああ、来てくださるんですか」と言った。
　Miss Yoshida の話では、

Miss Yoshida said that Mr. Lerner should have said

*Kyoo ikimasu.*

to mean "I'm coming today." But this didn't sound right to Mr. Lerner, because it seemed to imply that he was going away to some place other than Mr. Okada's office.

*          *          *

Basic words such as *kuru* and *iku* have various usages which can't be covered easily, so we will have to limit our discussion to specific instances. In cases when the speaker and the listener are at different locations and the speaker refers to his approaching the listener, *iku* is used in Japanese while an English speaker will say "I'm coming." In Japanese, when one goes away from where he is now, *iku* is used rather than *kuru*, regardless of whether or not one is going to where the listener is.

However, the verb *iku* is replaced by several other verbs when the speaker wants to be polite; he will use such expressions as *ukagaimasu, ojama-shimasu* or *mairimasu* to mean "I'm coming to where you are." So Mr. Lerner could have said *Kyoo ikimasu* as Miss Yoshida suggested, but to be more polite, he should have said

*Kyoo ukagaimasu*

or

*Kyoo ojama-shimasu.*

When Mr. Lerner said *Kyoo kuru-to omoimasu* in the above instance, Mr. Okada didn't understand him because it sounded as if someone or something was coming either to him or to Mr. Lerner. And the use of . . . *to omoimasu* (I think...) sounded as if Mr. Lerner was talking about someone or something else. To imply that he couldn't say definitely that he was

　　きょう行きます

と言うべきだったそうである。しかし Mr. Lerner にはこれは変な感じがした。「行きます」では、Mr. Okada の会社ではなく、ほかの所へ行ってしまうように聞こえるではないか……。

＊　　　　　　　＊　　　　　　　＊

　「来る」や「行く」のような基本的な語には、さまざま用法があって、簡単には説明しつくせない。ここでは特定の場合に限って話をする必要があろう。話し手と聞き手が別の所にいて、話し手が聞き手のほうへ近づくことを言うには、英語では "I'm coming" と言うが、日本語では「行きます」と言う。日本語の場合、現在いる所から離れることについては、聞き手がどこにいようとも、「行く」が用いられる。

　しかし、「行く」という動詞は、丁寧な話の中では別の動詞にかわってしまう。相手のいる所へ行くことは、「うかがいます」「おじゃまします」「参ります」のような表現で表される。上記の Mr. Lerner の場合、Miss Yoshida の言ったように「きょう行きます」と言ってもよいが、もっと丁寧な言いかたとしては、

　　きょううかがいます
　　きょうおじゃまします

と言うべきであった。

　上記の場合、Mr. Lerner が「キョウ来ルト思イマス」と言った時、Mr. Okada が理解しなかったのは、だれかがあるいは何かが、Mr. Okada あるいは Mr. Lerner のもとへ来るように聞こえたからである。また、「～ト思イマス」が、だれか他の人か何事かについて話しているという印象を与えたのである。Mr. Okada の都合がわからないうちは行くと明言できない、という気持ちを表すためには、

coming before he knew if it was all right with Mr. Okada, he could have said

*Kyoo ojama-shitai-n-desu-ga.*
(I'd like to come today.)

(December 9, 1979)

# *Chotto oshiete-kudasai*
## ちょっと 教えてください
### Please show me how to do it

A few days ago Mr. Lerner noticed that there was a new copying machine near Miss Yoshida's desk. He tried to copy some papers on it himself, but he did not know exactly how to work it, so he asked her

*Tsukaikata-ga wakarimasen-kara, chotto misete-kudasai.*

meaning "Since I don't know how to use it, please show me how to do it." Miss Yoshida took out a booklet from her desk, but before she had handed it to him, she realized what he meant, and said

*Tsukaikata-o oshiete-agemashoo-ka.*
(Shall I show you how to use it?)

Mr. Lerner thanked her, and realized that he still couldn't use the verb *oshieru* properly.

　　きょうおじゃましたいんですが

と言えばよかったのである。

# ちょっと教えてください

*Please show me how to do it*

　数日前、Mr. Lerner は Miss Yoshida の机のそばに新しいコピー機がおいてあるのを見た。そこで自分で書類をコピーしてみようとしたが、どう機械を動かすのかよくわからなかったので、

　　使イカタガワカリマセンカラ、チョット見セテクダサイ

と言った。Miss Yoshida は机の上から使用法のパンフレットを持ってきたが、それを渡す寸前に彼の言いたいことがわかったらしく、

　　使い方を教えてあげましょうか

と言った。Mr. Lerner は礼を言ったが、同時に、自分はまだ「教える」という動詞が正しく使えるようになっていないのだと気づいた……。

*　　　　　*　　　　　*

The verb *oshieru* has several meanings. One is "to teach" as in:

*Ima eego-o oshiete-imasu.*

(I'm teaching English now.)

Another meaning is "to show how to do something" as in:

*Eki-e iku michi-o oshiete-kudasai.*

(Please tell me the way to the station.)

When you want to know how to write a kanji, you should say

*Kono kanji-no kakikata-o oshiete-kudasai.*

(or *Kono kanji-wa doo kakeba ii-deshoo.*)

It can be understood but will sound strange to say

*Kono kanji-no kakikata-wa nan-desu-ka.*

When Mr. Lerner said . . . *misete-kudasai,* Miss Yoshida thought he was asking for a booklet or the like because *miseru* usually refers to showing something concrete, as in *hon-o miseru* (to show a book) or *tegami-o miseru* (to show a letter).

A third meaning of *oshieru* is "to give information," corresponding to the English word "tell." For instance when you want to know someone's address or phone number, *oshieru* is usually used as in:

*Juusho-o oshiete-kudasai.*

(Please tell me your address.)

*Denwa-bangoo-o oshiete-kudasaimasen-ka.*

(Will you please tell me your phone number?)

In these cases too, it sounds awkward to say *Juusho (Denwa-bangoo)-wa nan-desu-ka.*

(October 31, 1976)

　　　　　　＊　　　　　　＊　　　　　　＊

　「教える」という動詞にはいくつかの意味がある。ひとつは「教授する」こと
で、

　　　　今、英語を教えています

のように用いる。

　もうひとつの意味は「何かのやりかたを示す」ことで、

　　　　駅へ行く道を教えてください

のように使う。漢字の書きかたを知りたい時は、

　　　　この漢字の書きかたを教えてください

　　　　（または、この漢字はどう書けばいいでしょう。）

と言う。

　　　　コノ漢字ノ書キカタハ何デスカ

という言いかたは、理解はされるかもしれないが、違和感を与える。

　Mr. Lerner が「見セテクダサイ」と言った「見せる」は、「本を見せる」「手紙
を見せる」のように具体的な物について用いるので、Miss Yoshida は彼がパンフ
レットか何かをもとめているものだと思ってしまったのである。

　「教える」のもうひとつの意味は、「情報を与える」というもので、英語の
"tell" に対応する。たとえばだれかの住所や電話番号を知りたい時は「教える」
を使って、

　　　　住所を教えてください

　　　　電話番号を教えてくださいませんか

のように言うのが普通である。この場合にも、「住所（電話番号）ハ何デスカ」と
いうのは異様である。

（1976.10.31）

# *Kaku yoo-ni iwaremashita*
## 書く よう に 言われました
I was asked to write it

During lunchtime yesterday, Mr. Lerner was writing a Japanese composition that his Sensee had assigned him as homework. Miss Yoshida came by and asked what he was doing, so he explained that he was writing a composition and added

*Sensee-ga tanomimashita-kara.*

(Because my teacher asked me to do so.)

Miss Yoshida understood but he felt that his expression was not quite right. He changed it to

*Sensee-ni tanomaremashita-kara.*

(Because I was asked by my teacher.)

but she didn't seem satisfied. Mr. Lerner then wondered if the verb *tanomu* was wrong in this situation.

\*　　　　　\*　　　　　\*

A literal translation of the English sentence "My teacher asked me to write a composition" would be *Sensee-ga sakubun-o kaku koto-o tanomimashita*, but this is not appropriate. The verb *tanomu* is used to mean "to make a request" as in *Yoshida-san-ni shigoto-o tanomimashita* (I asked Miss Yoshida to work for me) or *Kaite kureru yoo-ni tanomimashita* (I asked her

# 書くように言われました

## I was asked to write it

　昨日の昼休みに Mr. Lerner は、先生から宿題として出された日本語の作文を書いていた。そこへ Miss Yoshida が来て何をしているのかとたずねたので、作文を書いていると答え、さらに、

　　　先生ガ頼ミマシタカラ

とつけ加えた。 Miss Yoshida がわかることはわかるがという顔をしたので、Mr. Lerner はまずかったのだろうと思い、

　　　先生ニ頼マレマシタカラ

と言い直したが、彼女はまだすっきりしない様子であった。「頼む」という動詞は合わないのかなと Mr. Lerner は思った……。

＊　　　　　＊　　　　　＊

　"My teacher asked me to write a composition." という英文を直訳すると、「先生ガ作文ヲ書クコトヲ頼ミマシタ」となるが、これは不適切である。「頼む」は、「依頼する」の意味で、「吉田さんに仕事を頼まれました」とか、「書いてくるように頼みました」のように用いられる。訓練上の必要なこととして何かをするように言う場合は、「頼む」は用いられない。教師が生徒に練習のために何か書くように命じたのなら、「先生が書くように言いました」と言うし、もっと丁寧な表現としては、「……書くようにおっしゃいました」と言う。あるいは話し手が

to write it for me). But when one tells someone to do what is required as a duty or training, the verb *tanomu* is not used. When a teacher has told his student to write something for practice, one says *Sensee-ga kaku yoo-ni iimashita*; more politely one says . . . *kaku yoo-ni osshaimashita*. Or if the speaker is a student he will often use the passive voice as in

. . . *kaku yoo-ni iwaremashita.*

(I was told to write it.)

If the teacher's request is made not for the sake of the student but for the teacher himself, *tanomu* is used as in

*Sensee-ni shigoto-no tetsudai-o tanomaremashita.*

(I was asked by my teacher to help him with his work.)

This implies that the teacher has asked the student to do such things as helping make teaching materials or repairing a tape recorder.

In the same way, when a boss tells someone to do something as part of his duties, . . . *yoo-ni yuu* is used, but when he has asked someone to help him personally, *tanomu* is used as in

*Eego-o oshiete-kureru yoo-ni tanomaremashita.*

(I was asked to teach him English.)

(August 31, 1980)

生徒であれば、受け身にして、

　　　……書くように言われました

とすることが多い。

　教師の依頼したことが、生徒のためになることでなく教師自身の利益になるのなら、「頼む」を使って、

　　　先生に仕事の手伝いを頼まれました

と言う。この文から想像されるのは、教師が生徒に教材の作成の手伝いやテープレコーダーの修理のようなことを頼んだ、ということである。

　同様に、上司が部下に業務として何かさせる場合には「〜ように言う」が用いられ、個人的な手伝いを頼んだ場合は、

　　　英語を教えてくれるように頼まれました

などと言う。

（1980.8.31）

# *Oboete-imasen*
## おぼえていません
### I don't remember

Mr. Lerner was talking about a movie that had been popular recently, but couldn't remember the name of the heroine, so he turned to Miss Yoshida for help saying

*Yoshida-san, oboemasen-ka.*

meaning "Don't you remember it, Miss Yoshida?" She didn't answer for a moment, and then said *Saa, nan-te itta-kashira* (Well, I wonder what her name was), and finally said

*Watashi-mo oboete-imasen.*
(I don't remember, either.)

Mr. Lerner realized then that he should have asked *oboete-imasen-ka* instead of *oboemasen-ka*, but he still couldn't help wondering how *oboeru* and *oboete-iru* are so different.

\*       \*       \*

While *oboete-iru* means "to remember," *oboeru* does not mean "remember" at all. It implies an effort to learn something and memorize it, as in

*Kanji-o oboeru-no-wa taihen-desu.*
(It is a lot of work to learn kanji.)

# おぼえていません

## *I don't remember*

Mr. Lerner は最近見た映画の話をしていたが、ヒロインの名前が思い出せなくなって、Miss Yoshida に助けてもらおうと思い、

　　吉田サン、オボエマセンカ

とたずねた。

彼女はすぐには返事をせずに考えていたが、やがて、「さあ、何て言ったかしら」と言い、ついに、

　　わたしもおぼえていません

と言った。それを聞いて、「オボエマセンカ」ではなく「おぼえていませんか」ときくべきだったのだ、とわかったが、それにしても「おぼえる」と「おぼえている」にはそんなに大きな違いがあるのだろうか、と Mr. Lerner は思った……。

＊　　　　　＊　　　　　＊

「おぼえている」は「記憶している」の意味であるが、「おぼえる」は「記憶している」の意味ではない。何かを学習し記憶しようと努力することを意味する。たとえば、

　　漢字をおぼえるのは大変です
　　なかなかおぼえられません

のように用いられる。

*Nakanaka oboeraremasen.*

(It is very difficult for me to memorize it.)

On the other hand, *oboete-iru* refers to the action of keeping something in one's memory, as in

*Sore-wa mada oboete-imasu.*

(I still remember that.)

*Komakai koto-wa oboete-imasen.*

(I don't remember the details.)

Thus, the two forms of the verb *oboeru* should be considered as having two different meanings—"to memorize" and "to remember."

But to refer to something not in one's memory, several expressions other than *oboete-iru* are very often used in daily conversation. When asked to recall someone's name, for instance, and unable to do so, one often says

*Saa, nan-te itta-deshoo.*

(Well, I wonder what his name was.)

*Nan-to yuu namae-deshita-kke.*

(I wonder what his name was.)

or

*Wasuremashita.*

(I forget.)

And when asking someone to remember something, one usually says

*Wasurenaide-kudasai.*

(Please don't forget it.)

rather than *oboete-ite-kudasai.* This is true of remembering to do something, too. To ask someone to remember to mail a letter, one usually says

*Yuubin-o dasu-no-o wasurenaide-kudasai.*

(Please don't forget to mail the letter.)

(January 4, 1981)

　他方、「おぼえている」は、何かの記憶を保持しているという行為をさす。た
とえば、

　　　それはまだおぼえています
　　　こまかいことはおぼえていません

のように言う。
　したがって、「おぼえる」と「おぼえている」は全く別の意味——「記憶にき
ざみこむ」(to memorize) と「記憶を保持する」(to remember)——にわかれると考
えたほうがよい。
　しかし、記憶にないということを表すには、「おぼえている」以外の表現も日
常よく使われる。だれかの名前を思い出してほしいと言われて思い出せない時な
どには、

　　　さあ、何て言ったでしょう
　　　何という名前でしたっけ

とか、

　　　忘れました

などと言う。
　人に記憶しておいてほしいと頼む時は、

　　　忘れないでください

が普通で、「おぼえていてください」は少ない。何かを忘れずに実行することに
ついては、なおさらそうである。手紙を必ず投函してほしいと頼む時などは、

　　　郵便を出すのを忘れないでください

がよく使われる。

（1981.1.4）

# Chapter 3

# Human Relations

人と人との関係

In this chapter we focus on expressions reflecting human relations and related situations. In other words politeness is our concern here. *Omochi-shimashoo, Itsu okaeshi-sureba yoroshii-deshoo, Kaite-kudasaimashita*— all these expressions indicate respect for the other's perspective. *Aa, are-desu-ka* is used when the speaker and the listener share common knowledge. *Chotto yuubinkyoku-e itte-kimasu* shows that the speaker will come back to where the listener is, rather than just telling where he is going. The use of *te-kuru* in this type of usage plays an important role in showing one's consideration toward others, although many Japanese speakers are not necessarily aware of that.

Reversing the subject and predicate, as in *Oishii-desu-ne, kono koohii*, is not a sign of clumsy sentence structure but an expression of intimacy with the listener. Saying just *Moo soro-soro dekakenai-to* and leaving out the rest is an indication of consideration in not pushing the listener. Saying *Yasumu wake-niwa ikanai* rather than *Yasumu koto-wa dekinai* implies that the speaker is conscious of other people.

Expressions referring to a wide range of quantity like *hodo, gurai, bakari* are also used to show consideration toward another person. These are not used in mathematics or at banks; they must be understood in terms of the situations. We have tried to clarify such points for readers.

この章では人と人の関係、またそれに付随する場面の問題からくる表現の違いをとりあげる。広い意味での丁寧さの表現がそのひとつである。「お持ちしましょう」「いつお返しすればよろしいでしょう」「書いてくださいました」などは相手の立場に敬意を示す表現である。「ああ、あれですか」は相手との共通の認識があることを示す表現であり、「ちょっと郵便局へ行ってきます」は「これから郵便局へ行きます」という情報伝達にとどまらず、話し手と聞き手の共存意識を表したものと考えることができる。こうした「てくる」などの用法は日本語の話し手が平生意識していないかもしれないが、聞き手に対する気持ちを表すものとして重要な役割を担っている。

　「おいしいですね、このコーヒー」は構文の間違いでなく相手に対する親近感を表すものであり、「もうそろそろ出かけないと……」と言ってあとを言わないのは、相手を追い詰めないという思いやりの表れである。「休むわけにはいかない」は「休むことができない」と違って心理的・社会的な要因が含まれ、他者に対する意識の反映が見られる。

　なお、「ぐらい、ほど、ばかり」のような幅のある数の示し方を単にあいまいとしてかたづける安易な解釈でなく、相手への配慮の表れであることを説いた。数学の授業や銀行での会話では使われない概数がどんな場合に使われるか、人と人との関係、場面との関係で語句を考える態度で必要であることを明らかにした。

# *Aa, are-desu-ka*
## ああ、あれですか
*Oh, is it that?*

One afternoon Miss Yoshida came to Mr. Lerner and asked if he could join the picnic she was planning. While she was explaining her plan, Mr. Takada passed by and asked what she was talking about. She said,

*Are-desu.*
(About that. —lit., It is that.)

Then Mr. Takada said,

*Aa, are-desu-ka.*
(Oh, about that? —lit., Oh, is it that?)

She never mentioned the picnic or her plan in this exchange, but he immediately understood anyway.

*　　　　*　　　　*

Such words as *kore* "this," *sore* "that," *are* "that over there," and *dore* "which one" are used to point out things the speaker wants to refer to. Most textbooks explain that *kore* is used to refer to things close to the speaker and *sore* to things close to the listener, and *are* is used to refer to things far from both the speaker and the listener. This explanation is correct so far as the question of space is concerned, but you must keep in mind that the relation between the speaker and the listener and the thing

# ああ、あれですか

*Oh, is it that?*

ある日の午後、Mr. Lerner のところへ Miss Yoshida が来て、ピクニックに行こうと思うんだけど行きませんかと誘った。その予定の説明をしているところへ Mr. Takada が通りかかって、何の話かとたずねた。Miss Yoshida は、

> あれです

と言った。すると Mr. Takada も、

> ああ、あれですか

と言った。ピクニックとも予定ともひと言も言わないのに、それでわかってしまうのだろうか……。

＊　　　　　＊　　　　　＊

「これ」「それ」「あれ」「どれ」は、話し手が自分の言いたいことを指すのに用いる。大抵の教科書は、「これ」は話し手に近いものを、「それ」は聞き手に近いものを、「あれ」は話し手からも聞き手からも遠いものを指す、と説明している。この説明は、空間の問題に関する限り正しいが、ここで忘れてならないのは、話し手と指すものとの物理的な距離関係よりも、指すものをめぐる話し手と聞き手の人間関係のほうが重要だということである。

たとえば「あれ」は、話し手と聞き手が話題について知識を共有する、ということを前提としている。聞き手が知らない話題については、「あれ」ではなく

referred to is even more important than the physical distance between the speaker and the thing he refers to.

For instance, *are* presupposes that the speaker and the listener share a knowledge of the subject matter. When the listener has no knowledge of the subject matter, *sore* is used instead of *are*.

The knowledge of the subject matter does not have to be acquired through sight. When someone hears a strange noise outside the room, he says to a person in the same room *Are-wa nan-desu-ka* (What is that?) because both the speaker and the listener have heard the noise and thereby acquired a common knowledge of it.

The knowledge does not have to be gained through personal experience, either. The picture of Mona Lisa is usually referred to as *are* even if the speaker or the listener have not seen it because it is known to both of them. But if you talk about some picture unknown to the listener, *sore* is used.

Since how often *are* is used roughly corresponds to the amount of knowledge the speaker and the listener share, you will hear it more often among family members and among coworkers. Couples who have been married a long time naturally tend to use it quite often. A happily married husband is very likely to say to his wife,

*Are-o motte-kite.*
(Bring me that.)

And she will bring exactly what he wants.

(November 21, 1976)

「それ」を用いる。

　話題について知識を持つということは、必ずしも目に見えるということではない。部屋の外で何か変な音がしたら、同じ部屋にいる人に「あれは何ですか」とたずねる。自分も相手もその音を聞き、共通の知識を得たからである。

　また、その知識は直接体験して得るとは限らない。モナ・リザの絵などは、お互いに見たことがなくても有名なものだから、普通「あれ」と言う。しかし、聞き手が知らない絵について話す時は、「それ」と言う。

　「あれ」が使われる頻度は、話し手と聞き手の共有する知識の量に比例するから、家族の間や同僚の間では頻度が高くなる。したがって結婚してから長い夫婦などは、「あれ」を使う回数が多い。幸福な結婚生活を送っている夫は妻に、

　　　あれを持ってきて

と言い、妻は誤たずその物を持ってくる、ということになる。

（1976.11.21）

# *Oishii-desu-ne, kono koohii*
## おいしいですね、このコーヒー
### It's good, this coffee

A few weeks ago Mr. Lerner had a cup of coffee at a little coffee shop with Miss Yoshida. After tasting the coffee, Miss Yoshida remarked

*Oishii-desu-ne, kono koohii.*
(lit., It's good, this coffee.)

He agreed, but thought to himself that he would have said

*Kono koohii-wa oishii-desu-ne.*

without reversing the order of the subject and the predicate. When he asked her if she would like another cup, she said

*Iie, juubun-desu, ippai-de.*
(lit., No, it's enough, with one cup.)

reversing the order of the phrases again.

After that he paid special attention to the conversations around him, and noticed that this type of inversion is used very often. And he also realized that he himself had never done this; he wondered if he should sometimes try it when speaking Japanese.

*       *       *

In daily conversation the Japanese often reverse the order of the subject

# おいしいですね、このコーヒー

## *It's good, this coffee*

　数週間前のこと、Mr. Lerner は Miss Yoshida と一緒に小さな喫茶店でコーヒーを飲んだ。コーヒーをひと口飲んでから Miss Yoshida は、

　　おいしいですね、このコーヒー

と言った。Mr. Lerner は同意したが、自分だったら主語と述語を逆にしないで、

　　このコーヒーはおいしいですね

と言っただろうと思った。もう 1 杯どうかとたずねると彼女は、

　　いいえ、十分です、1 杯で

と、また主述を逆転させて答えた。

　その後 Mr. Lerner は周囲の人々の話しかたに注意していたが、この種の逆転が極めて頻繁に行われることがわかった。同時に、自分では一度もそうしたことがないのにも気づいた。日本語をしゃべる時は、たまにはこの逆転をやったほうがいいのだろうか……。

　　　　　　　*　　　　　　　*　　　　　　　*

　日常の会話では、日本人は主語とその他の部分の順序をよく逆にする。あるいは、普通なら文の最後に来る部分から、文を始めたりする。厳密に言えば、語順は自由に変えることはできないが、句の順は変えられるのだ。つまり、「ですね、

and the rest of the sentence, or start their sentences with what usually comes last. Strictly speaking, the word order does not change freely but the order of phrases can be changed; you can say *Oishii-desu-ne, kono koohii*, but you cannot say *Desu-ne oishii, koohii kono*. In fact, you will often hear such sentences as:

> *Ii otenki-desu-ne, kyoo-wa.*
> (lit., It's a fine day, today.)
> *Yokatta-desu-ne, ano eega.*
> (lit., It was good, that movie.)
> *Kimashita-yo, henji-ga.*
> (lit., It came, the reply.)

By inversing the order in this way, you can give an impression of familiarity and enthusiasm. Because of this, inversion is most often used in speech that expresses one's emotions such as surprise, criticism, excitement, evaluation and the like. It is usually avoided in formal speech as well as in written language.

Foreigners may not feel it's correct to say sentences like *Oishii-desu-ne, kono koohii,* but they could first try such inversion as giving an explanation after the main sentence. For example, when one wants to say "Please wait a moment. I'll come in a minute," one can say either

> *Sugu modorimasu-kara matte-ite-kudasai.*
> (lit., Because I'm coming back in a minute, please wait.)

or

> *Chotto matte-ite-kudasai, sugu modorimasu-kara.*

Both are correct, but the second sentence sounds more conversational.

(May 14, 1978)

おいしい、このコーヒー」とは言えないが、「おいしいですね、このコーヒー」
は言えるのである。実際、次のような文はよく聞かれる。

> いいお天気ですね、きょうは
> よかったですね、あの映画
> 来ましたよ、返事が

　このように順を変えることによって、語の調子に親しみと熱意を加えることが
できる。このため、こうした逆転は、驚き、批判、興奮、評価、その他、話し手
の感情を表す時に、最もよく用いられるのである。改まった話しかたや、文書の
文には、こうしたことは行われない。
　外国人にとっては、「おいしいですね、このコーヒー」のような文は正しくな
いと感じられるかもしれない。しかし、主体となる文のあとに説明的に加える形
で、この逆転を試みてみるのも一案である。たとえば、"Please wait a moment.
I'll come in a minute." と言う場合、

> すぐ戻りますから、待っていてください

とも、

> ちょっと待っていてください、すぐ戻りますから

とも言う。どちらも正しい。しかし後者のほうが会話的である。

（1978.5.14）

# *'Doozo'* -to *'Onegai-shimasu'*
# 「どうぞ」と「おねがいします」

### *'Please'* vs. *'I request it'*

The other day Mr. Lerner visited Mr. Okada at his office. When he arrived, Mr. Okada was not in his room, and his secretary took him to the room where he was working. She asked Mr. Lerner to follow her, saying

*Kochira-e onegai-shimasu.*

He understood that she meant "Please come this way." He had learned that in polite expressions such verbs as "come" and "go" are often left out if they can be understood from the situation. But this expression *Kochira-e onegai-shimasu* was not familiar to him. He wondered if she could have said *Kochira-e doozo* instead.

*      *      *

When making requests politely, *onegai-shimasu* is often used without explicitly indicating an action. To ask someone to write down his name, for example, one often says

*Koko-ni onegai-shimasu.*

meaning "Please write it here." Verbs other than "write" can also be left out; *Koko-ni onegai-shimasu* can mean *Koko-ni oite-kudasai* (Please put it here) or *Koko-ni tsukete-kudasai* (Please attach it here), too.

*Doozo* is also used without a verb as in *Kochira-e doozo* (Please come

# 「どうぞ」と「お願いします」

## *'Please' vs. 'I request it'*

先日 Mr. Lerner は Mr. Okada の会社を訪ねたが、到着した時 Mr. Okada は自分の部屋にいなかった。秘書が彼の執務中の部屋へ案内してくれることになり、

　　　こちらへお願いします

と言った。これが "Please come this way." の意味であることはわかった。丁寧な表現では、「来る」とか「行く」という動詞は場面からわかる場合は省かれる。しかし、この「こちらへお願いします」は初めて聞く言いかただった。「こちらへどうぞ」と言っても同じだろうか、と Mr. Lerner は思った……。

＊　　　　　　＊　　　　　　＊

丁寧な依頼の場合、実際の動作をあからさまに言わず、ただ「お願いします」と言うことがよくある。たとえば名前を書いてもらいたい時、"Please write it here." の意味で、

　　　ここへお願いします

とよく言う。「書く」以外の動詞にも省かれるものがある。「ここにお願いします」と言えば、「ここに置いてください」の場合もあるし、「ここに付けてください」の場合もある。

「どうぞ」もまた、動詞を省いて「こちらへどうぞ」とか「こちらにどうぞ」のように使われる。

this way) or *Kochira-ni doozo* (Please write it here) or (Please put it here).

The difference between the two is that while *onegai-shimasu* implies a request (it is derived from *negau,* to ask or to implore), *doozo* implies a recommendation as to the means of achieving the listener's wishes. Therefore *doozo* is appropriate in such cases as showing a visitor to the reception room or asking someone to sit down. On the other hand, *onegai-shimasu* is used to ask someone to do a favor. Mr. Okada's secretary used *onegai-shimasu* because she felt that she was asking a favor of Mr. Lerner in taking him to another room. Another person might have used *doozo* in the same situation.

(June 21, 1981)

# *Ashi-o fumaremashita*
## 足を ふまれました
### Someone stepped on my foot

Mr. Lerner had to take an especially crowded train to the office yesterday morning. When he arrived at the office, he was tired and was resting a while before starting his work. Miss Yoshida asked him if he was all right, so he explained that the train had been crowded, and added

*Dareka-ga ashi-o fumimashita.*
(Someone stepped on my foot.)

Then he remembered that the passive form is more appropriate and said

「どうぞ」と「お願いします」との違いは、「お願いします」のほうは依頼を示す（「願う」という動詞から来ている）のに対し、「どうぞ」は相手が自分の希望を達成する手段を推薦するという意味合いをもつ。したがって、「どうぞ」は客を応接室に案内したり、椅子をすすめたりする場合に適切である。それに対し「お願いします」は、相手に恩恵を乞うものである。Mr. Okada の秘書が「お願いします」を使ったのは、Mr. Lerner にほかの部屋へ足を運んでもらうという恩恵を乞うと感じたからである。同じ場面でも別の人だったら「どうぞ」と言ったかもしれない。

(1981.6.21)

# 足をふまれました

*Someone stepped on my foot*

きのうの朝 Mr. Lerner は、やむを得ず、ひどくこんだ電車に乗った。会社に着いた時はすっかり疲れてしまい、仕事を始める前にひと休みしていた。Miss Yoshida がどこか悪いのかときいたので、満員電車に乗ったことを話し、

　　　ダレカガ足ヲフミマシタ

とつけ加えた。

　そのあと、受身の形のほうがよいだろうと思いなおして、

*Ashi-ga fumaremashita.*
(My foot was stepped on.)

Miss Yoshida immediately understood but said he should have said

*Ashi-o fumaremashita.*

instead.

*        *        *

In conversational Japanese the passive form is used to indicate that someone has been affected by the action of someone else as in

*(Watashi-wa) kachoo-ni shikararemashita.*
(I was scolded by the section chief.)
*(Watashi-wa) okane-o nusumaremashita.*
(I had my money stolen.)

In the above sentences, *Watashi-wa* is left out when it can be understood from the situation, but in such passive sentences the subject must be the person who suffers from the action of someone else rather than the person's belongings. Therefore you can say either

*Watashi-wa ashi-o fumaremashita.*

or

*Ashi-o fumaremashita.*

when someone has stepped on your foot, but it sounds strange to say

*Ashi-ga fumaremashita.*
(My foot was stepped on.)

　　　足ガフマレマシタ

と言った。Miss Yoshida はすぐ理解したが、やはり、

　　　足をふまれました

のほうがいいと言った……。

＊　　　　　　＊　　　　　　＊

　日本語の話しことばの受身は、だれかほかの人の行為によって影響を受けたことを示すのに用いられる。たとえば、

　　　（わたしは）課長にしかられました
　　　（わたしは）お金をぬすまれました

のように言う。上の例の場合、周囲の状況からわかる場合は「わたし」は言わないが、主語を示す場合、それはだれかの行為によって影響をうける人であって、その人の持ち物や体の一部を主語にすることはない。つまり、

　　　わたしは足をふまれました

とか、

　　　足をふまれました

とは言うが、

　　　足がふまれました

は奇異にひびくのである。

　同時に、納めたくもない税金を納めるはめになった場合、

In the same way, when you have had to pay taxes against your will, you will say

*Zeekin-o torareta.*
(lit., I had my taxes taken.)

rather than

*Zeekin-ga torareta.*
(lit., My taxes were taken.)

(May 30, 1982)

# *Chotto yuubinkyoku-e itte-kimasu*
## ちょっと 郵便局へ いってきます
### *I'm going to the post office*

Mr. Lerner asked Sensee how he could make his Japanese sound more natural. Sensee suggested that he use two verbs together—for instance, saying *itte-kimasu* (lit., I'll go and come back) instead of *ikimasu* or *yonde-mimasu* (lit., I'll read and see) instead of *yomimasu*.

So he started to pay more attention to this in the conversations of the people around him. Yesterday afternoon he heard Miss Yoshida say

*Chotto yuubinkyoku-e itte-kimasu-kedo . . .*
(I'm going to the post office. —lit., I'll go to the post office for a short
  while and come back, but . . .)

　　　税金をとられた

とは言うが、

　　　税金がとられた

とは言わないのである。

（1982.5.30）

# ちょっと郵便局へ行ってきます

*I'm going to the post office*

　Mr. Lerner は先生に、もっと自然な日本語を話すにはどうしたらいいかとたずねた。先生は、動詞を２つ重ねて使うといいと言った。たとえば、「行きます」の代わりに「行ってきます」、「読みます」の代わりに「読んでみます」と言う、ということであった。

　そこで Mr. Lerner は周囲の人の話を聞く時、この点に気をつけるようにした。昨日の午後も、Miss Yoshida が、

　　　ちょっと郵便局へ行ってきますけど……

と言うのに気がついた。

He had learned that *itte-kimasu* is used when the speaker wants to emphasize his intention of coming back, but had not used it himself and had not paid much attention to it before.

Then Mr. Takada said to Miss Yoshida

*Ja, kono tegami-mo dashite-kite-moraeru?*

(Then will you mail this letter for me? —lit., Then can I receive the favor of your mailing this letter too and then coming back?)

Mr. Lerner was surprised that Mr. Takada had used three, not two, verbs together—*dasu* (to mail), *kuru* (to come) and *morau* (to receive); he felt that if he had to learn this type of expression he really had a long way to go.

*　　　　*　　　　*

Using two verbs together is very common in daily conversation, and being able to do so helps make one's Japanese more expressive. Such expressions as *itte-kimasu* are made up of two verbs; *iku* is used here as the main verb and *kuru* as the helping verb, although any verb can be used as the main one. While the main verb is used to indicate the action, the helping verb expresses the intention or the mental attitude of the speaker or the doer. For instance, when one says

*Yonde-mimasu.*

(I'll read it and see how it is.)

*yomu* refers to the action while *miru* is used to indicate the speaker's interest in the result of the action. In a similar way when one says

*Osoku natte-shimatta.*

(I was late.)

「行ってきます」というのは、行ってまた戻るという意志を強調するものだということは、すでに学んでいたが、自分で使うこともなかったし、人が使うのにも気がついていなかったのである。

　すると Mr. Takada が Miss Yoshida に、

　　じゃ、この手紙も出してきてもらえる？

と言った。「出す」「くる」「もらう」と、実に３つも動詞を重ねて使っているではないか。こんな言いかたができるようになるのは、まだまだ先のことだろうなと、Mr. Lerner は思った……。

＊　　　　　＊　　　　　＊

　２つの動詞を重ねて使うことは日常の話でよく行われる。これができると、日本語の表現が豊かになる。「行ってきます」は２つの動詞からできているが、「行く」は主要な動詞、「くる」は補助的な動詞として使われている。（どの動詞も主要動詞として使うことはできる。）主要動詞は動作を示し、補助動詞は話し手や行為者の意図や心的態度を表す。たとえば、

　　読んでみます

という時、「読む」は動作を指し、「みる」はその行為の結果に対する話し手の関心を表す。同様に、

　　おそくなってしまった

では、「しまう」は話し手の不本意な気持ちを示す。

　「もらう」「いただく」「あげる」「くれる」「くださる」は、他の動詞に加えられて、話し手が人に好意的な行為をしたり、人から好意を受けたりすることを示す。そこで、時には Mr. Takada が使った「出してきてもらう」のように、３つの動詞が続くこともある。

the use of *shimau* implies that the speaker regrets what he has done.

Such verbs as *morau, itadaku* (to receive), *ageru* (to give), *kureru* (to give me) and *kudasaru* (to give me) are added to other verbs to indicate the speaker's giving or receiving a favor from someone. Thus you will sometimes hear three verbs together as in *dashite-kite-morau* which Mr. Takada used or as in:

*Yonde-mite-itadakemasu-ka.*
(Will you read this and see how it is? —lit., Can I receive the favor of your reading it and seeing?)

(February 19, 1978)

# *Tsuide-ni*
## ついでに
### *While...*

Yesterday afternoon Miss Yoshida told Mr. Lerner and Mr. Takada that she was going to the post office and asked if they wanted her to buy anything for them. Then Mr. Takada said

*Ja, tsuide-ni tabako katte-kite-kudasai.*
(Then will you buy me some cigarettes on the way?)

Mr. Lerner realized that he had once learned the expression *tsuide-ni* and had heard it used many times, but that he had never used it himself. He knew that *tsuide-ni* refers to doing something while doing something

読んでみていただけますか

のように。

> ▶英語などでは、助動詞 will、can などは別として、動詞を２つ続けて
> 使うことはないので、この補助動詞は特に訓練をしないと、なかなか
> 使えるようにならない。特に補助動詞は心的態度に関係するため、事
> 実関係だけでなく、話し手の気持ちを重視する学習態度が必要とな
> る。

（1978.2.19）

# ついでに

### *While . . .*

　　昨日の午後 Miss Yoshida が Mr. Lerner と Mr. Takada に、これから郵便局に行くけど何か買ってきてほしいものはないかとたずねた。すると Mr. Takada は、

　　じゃ、ついでにたばこ買ってきてください

と言った。

　　「ついでに」という表現はもう習ったし、何回も聞いたことがあるが、自分で使ったことはなかった、と Mr. Lerner は思った。「ついでに」というのは、何かをしながらほかのことをする、たとえば郵便局へ行きながらたばこを買う、とい

else, as buying cigarettes while going to the post office, but he was not sure which action should be done first or whether the order didn't matter.

*      *      *

The word *tsuide* fundamentally means "next" or "of second importance"; *tsuide-ni . . . suru* means "to do something of second importance, taking advantage of a chance to do something." For instance, in Miss Yoshida's case, going to the post office is the business of the first importance for her, and buying cigarettes for Mr. Takada is second in importance. It does not matter whether she buys the cigarettes on her way to the post office or on her way back; what matters is which action is more important.

This expression *tsuide-ni* is often used when asking someone to do a favor in a reserved way; it is considerate to assume that one's request should not be regarded as first in importance. Thus, one often uses this expression to ask a person going out on business to do something, as in

*Tsuide-ni kono tegami dashite-kudasai.*
(Please mail this letter for me while you're out.)

Sometimes *tsuide-ga attara* (lit., if you have a chance to do something of second importance) or *tsuide-no toki-ni* (lit., when you have a chance to do something of second importance) is used in social situations when asking a favor to show one's reserve, as in

A: *Itsu okaeshi-sureba yoroshii-deshoo.*
(When would you like me to return it?)
B: *Ie, itsu-demo kekkoo-desu.*
(Any time will do.)
A: *Soo-desu-ka. Demo . . .*
(Well, . . .)

うような時に使うのだと思ったが、どちらの行為が先なのか、順序はどうでもよいのか、そのへんが疑問だった……。

＊　　　　　＊　　　　　＊

「ついで」という語は基本的には「次」とか「第２位」の意味で、「ついでに〜する」というのは、「何かをする機会を利用して次位の意義をもつ行為を行う」ということである。たとえば Miss Yoshida の場合、郵便局へ行くことが第一の用件であり、Mr. Takada のためにたばこを買うことはそれに次ぐものである。買うのは郵便局へ行く道でも帰り道でもかまわない。問題になるのは、どちらの行為のほうが大事かということである。

この「ついでに」という表現は、遠慮がちに人にものを頼む時によく用いられる。自分の頼みが第一の重要性をもつと見なされてはならないとすることは、相手に対する礼儀である。したがって、よく使われるのは、何かの用があって出かけようとする人に、

　　　　ついでにこの手紙を出してください

と頼むような場合である。

「ついでがあったら」とか「ついでの時に」という表現も、遠慮がちに人にものを頼む場合によく用いられる。

　　　　Ａ：いつお返しすればよろしいでしょう
　　　　Ｂ：いえ、いつでもけっこうです
　　　　Ａ：そうですか、でも……
　　　　Ｂ：いつかおついでの時にお持ちください

のように言う。これは、相手はその目的のためにだけ「わざわざ」来なくても、何かほかの目的で訪ねてくる時に持ってきてくれればよい、という思いやりの表現なのである。

（1981.1.25）

B: *Itsuka otsuide-no toki-ni omochi-kudasai.*

(Please bring it when you happen to come by.)

This implies that the listener does not have to come for that purpose alone (*wazawaza*), but that he can bring it when he is visiting the speaker for some other purpose.

(January 25, 1981)

# *Omochi-shimashoo*
## お持ちしましょう
### Let me carry it for you

A few days ago Mr. Mori, the director of the company, was carrying a cassette tape recorder from one room to another. Mr. Takada saw him and said

*Rekoodaa, omochi-shimashoo.*

(Let me carry the tape recorder for you.)

Mr. Lerner remembered that he had learned that it is more polite to say *omochi-shimashoo* than to say *motte-agemashoo*, and thought that he should use this expression some time.

The next day, he saw an elderly woman on the platform waiting for the train carrying a heavy bag, and offered to help her saying

*Nimotsu-o mochi-shimashoo.*

# お持ちしましょう

*Let me carry it for you*

　2、3日前、社長の Mr. Mori がテープレコーダーを持って、隣の部屋へ移ろうとしているのを見た Mr. Takada は、

　　レコーダー、お持ちしましょう

と声をかけた。Mr. Lerner は、「持ってあげましょう」より「お持ちしましょう」のほうが丁寧であると習ったのを思い出し、自分もいつか使ってみようと思った。

　次の日、駅のプラットフォームで電車を待っている初老の婦人が、大きなかばんを持っているのを見たので、

　　荷物ヲ　モチシマショウ

meaning "I will carry your luggage for you." The woman thanked him, but she hesitated before doing so, and Mr. Lerner suspected that he hadn't said the expression correctly.

*       *       *

When offering to help, it is all right to say *motte-agemashoo*, but this expression is not very polite. To seniors or older people, it is recommended that you say *omochi-shimashoo* instead. This expression is formed by adding *o* and *suru* to the stem of verbs. Mr. Lerner was right when he tried to say *Nimotsu-o omochi-shimashoo*, but he left out the *o* in *omochi-shimashoo*, and so his sentence sounded strange. The particle *o* in *nimotsu-o* can be left out in conversation, so Mr. Takada said *Rekoodaa, omochi-shimashoo*, but the *o* in *omochi-shimashoo* should not be left out.

It might be helpful to practice expressions such as the following which are used very often in offering help or making a proposal.

*otodoke-shimashoo* (I'll bring or deliver it)
—from the verb *todokeru*
*otsutae-shimashoo* (I'll tell him)
—from the verb *tsutaeru*
*oshirase-shimashoo* (I'll let you know)
—from the verb *shiraseru*

It requires careful practice when two *o*'s are used successively as in

*ooshie-shimashoo* (I'll tell you)
—from the verb *oshieru*
*ookuri-shimashoo* (I'll send it to you, or I'll go with you)
—from the verb *okuru*

(February 25, 1979)

と言った。婦人はややためらってからお礼を言った。この言いかたはまずかったのだろうか……。

＊　　　　　＊　　　　　＊

　助力を申し出る時、「持ってあげましょう」と言ってもよいが、これはあまり丁寧ではない。目上の人や年長の人には、「お持ちしましょう」と言ったほうが適切である。この表現は動詞の語幹に「お〜する」をつけて作るのであるから、Mr. Lerner が「荷物をお持ちしましょう」と言おうとしたのは、正しかったのであるが、「お持ちしましょう」の「お」を落としてしまったので、変に聞こえたのである。「荷物を」の「を」は会話ではよく省かれる。Mr. Takada も「テープレコーダー、お持ちしましょう」と言った。だが「お持ちしましょう」の「お」は省いてはいけないのである。

　助力を申し出る時や提案をする時によく使われる、次のような表現を練習しておくとよいだろう。

　　　お届けしましょう
　　　お伝えしましょう
　　　お知らせしましょう

"o" の音が２つ続く時は、特に注意深く練習する必要がある。

　　　お教えしましょう
　　　お送りしましょう

などである。

（1979.2.25）

# *Itsu okaeshi-sureba yoroshii-deshoo*
## いつ おかえしすれば よろしいでしょう
### *When would you like me to return it?*

Mr. Mori, the director of the company, has a fine collection of wood-block prints, and Mr. Lerner wanted to borrow some of them for a few days. He asked Mr. Mori

*Itsu kaeshite-moraitai-desu-ka.*

to mean "When would you like me to return them?" Mr. Mori didn't answer for a moment, and then said he would like to have them back within a week. When Mr. Lerner told Miss Yoshida about this, she said that he should have said

*Itsu okaeshi-sureba yoroshii-deshoo.*

(lit., When will it be all right for me to return them?)

instead. Mr. Lerner wondered if there was no expression in Japanese corresponding to the English "Would you like me to . . . ?"

*          *          *

To politely ask someone's wishes, the form . . . *tai-desu-ka* or . . . *te-moraitai-desu-ka* should be avoided, because . . . *tai* does not express politeness and is mainly used with the first person or with the second person when one does not have to be polite.

One usually asks someone's wishes politely with . . . *shimashoo-ka* or . . . *sureba yoroshii-deshoo*; in both cases the subject of the sentence is the speaker, as in

# いつお返しすればよろしいでしょう

*When would you like me to return it?*

　社長の Mr. Mori が木版画のすばらしいコレクションをもっていると聞いて、Mr. Lerner はその何枚かを 2、3 日貸してもらいたいと思い、

　　　イツ返シテモライタイデスカ

とたずねた。Mr. Mori はちょっと黙っていたが、やがて、1 週間ぐらいで返してほしいと答えた。Miss Yoshida にこの話をすると、そういう言いかたでなく、

　　　いつお返しすればよろしいでしょう

と言うべきだったのだと言った。日本語には英語の "Would you like me to . . . ?" に当たる表現がないのだろうか、と Mr. Lerner は思った……。

　　　　　　＊　　　　　　　＊　　　　　　　＊

　人の希望を丁寧にたずねる時は、「〜たいですか」や「〜てもらいたいですか」は避けるべきである。「たい」には敬意が含まれず、話し手に関することや丁寧に話す必要のない相手に対して用いられる。

　人の意向を丁寧にたずねる時は、「〜しましょうか」あるいは「〜すればよろしいでしょうか」が通常用いられる。どちらの場合も文の主語は話し手であって、

*Kono tsugi-wa itsu ukagai-*(or *mairi-)mashoo-ka.*
(When should I come next time?)
*Kono tsugi-wa itsu ukagaeba yoroshii-deshoo.*
(When should I come next time?)

> (*Maireba* sounds old-fashioned.)

To ask someone politely "When would you like to have it?" there are such expressions as

*Itsu motte-kureba yoroshii-deshoo.*
(lit., When will it be all right for me to bring it?)
*Itsu motte-agareba yoroshii-deshoo.*

> (The same as above, but this sounds more humble.)

*Itsu owatashi-sureba yoroshii-deshoo.*
(lit., When will it be good for me to hand it over to you?)

Saying *Itsu tsukaitai-desu-ka* (When do you want to use it?) or *Itsu hoshii-desu-ka* (When do you want it?) sounds blunt and awkward. It is better to use such expressions as

*Itsu oiriyoo-desu-ka.*
(lit., When would be needing it?)
*Itsu otsukai-ni narimasu-ka.*
(lit., When would be using it?)

(January 18, 1981)

この次はいつうかがいましょうか／〜まいりましょうか

この次はいつうかがえばよろしいでしょう

　　（「まいれば」はやや古風にひびく）

のように言う。

　英語の "When would you like to have it ?" の意味を表す丁寧な表現としては、

いつ持ってくればよろしいでしょう

いつ持って上がればよろしいでしょうか

　　（「上がれば」のほうが謙譲の度が強い）

いつお渡しすればよろしいでしょう

などがある。

　「いつ使いたいですか」とか「いつほしいですか」と言うのは、ぶっきらぼう
で不適切である。

いつお入り用ですか

いつお使いになりますか

などのほうがよい。

（1981.1.18）

# *Kaite-kudasaimashita*
## 書いてくださいました
### *He kindly wrote it for me*

Professor Takahashi is a good calligrapher, so Mr. Lerner asked him to write something for him. The professor first declined, saying that he was not that good, but finally wrote the Chinese character meaning "perseverance" for him with a big brush. Mr. Lerner liked it very much and hung it on the wall behind his desk at the office. Miss Yoshida immediately noticed it and asked about it, so he explained saying

*Takahashi-sensee-ga kaite-kudasaimashita.*
(Professor Takahashi kindly wrote it for me.)

But at the same time he wondered if he should have said

*Takahashi-sensee-ni kaite-itadakimashita.*
(lit., I received from Professor Takahashi the favor of writing it.)

He had learned that both expressions meant the same thing, but wondered if there wasn't some difference between them.

*   *   *

The two expressions . . . *ga kudasaimashita* and . . . *ni itadakimashita* are used to describe the same action: someone giving something, usually to the speaker. When someone has done some action for the speaker, he can say either . . . *ga* . . . *te-kudasaimashita* or . . . *ni* . . . *te-itadakimashita*: The

# 書いてくださいました

*He kindly wrote it for me*

Professor Takahashi はすばらしい書家である。そこで Mr. Lerner は何か一筆書いてほしいと頼んだ。教授ははじめはそんなにうまくないからと断ったが、ついには「忍耐」という意味の漢字を太い筆で書いてくれた。 Mr. Lerner は喜んで、それを会社の机の後ろの壁にかけた。すると Miss Yoshida が目ざとく見つけ、質問してきたので、

　　　　高橋先生ガ書イテクダサイマシタ

と答えた。しかし、そう言いながら、むしろ、

　　　　高橋先生に書いていただきました

と言うべきではなかったのかと思った。

　この2つの表現は同じ意味を表すと習ったが、2つの間には何か違いがあるのではなかろうか、と彼は思った……。

＊　　　　　　＊　　　　　　＊

「～がくださいました」と「～にいただきました」は、同じ行為を言っている。だれかが何かを、通常は話し手に、与えたという意味である。だれかが話し手のために何らかの行為をした場合、「～が～てくださいました」とも「～に～ていただきました」とも言う。それほど丁寧でない場合の「くれました」「もらいました」についても、同様である。

less polite expressions *kuremashita* and *moraimashita* are also used in the same way.

Both . . . *ga kaite-kudasaimashita* and . . . *ni kaite-itadakimashita* are used to express the speaker's gratitude toward the person who has written something for him. Mr. Lerner could have said . . . *ni kaite-itadakimashita* as well as . . . *ga kaite-kudasaimashita*. The speaker's attitude is, however, different in the two expressions. When saying . . . *ga kaite-kudasaimashita*, the speaker emphasizes the writer's being kind, whereas when he says . . . *ni kaite-itadakimashita* he is more concerned with himself having received a favor. Thus if one were to distinguish between the two expressions,

*Sensee-ga kaite-kudasaimashita.*

corresponds to "He kindly wrote it for me," whereas

*Sensee-ni kaite-itadakimashita.*

corresponds to "I received from him the favor of writing it." The expression used depends on the situation or how the speaker wants to describe the fact.

(August 16, 1981)

　「～が書いてくださいました」も「～に書いていただきました」も、ともに何か書いてくれた人に対する感謝を示すのに用いられる。上記の Mr. Lerner の場合、「～が書いてくださいました」と「～に書いていただきました」のいずれでも使える。

　しかし、この2つの間には話し手の態度の違いがある。「～が書いてくださいました」と言うと書いた人の親切さを強調するが、「～に書いていただきました」の場合、話し手は自分が恩恵を受けたことを強調している。したがって、この2つを区別しようとするなら、

　　　先生が書いてくださいました

は "He kindly wrote it for me." に当たり、

　　　先生に書いていただきました

は "I received from him the favor of writing it." に当たるであろう。どちらを使うかは、その場の状況や話し手の表現の態度によって決まってくる。

（1981.8.16）

# *Kaettara sugu denwa-shimasu*
## かえったらすぐ電話します
*I'll call you as soon as I get home*

Mr. Takada wanted to have dinner with Mr. Lerner to introduce him to one of his friends, so he asked what evening he would be free the following week. But Mr. Lerner had left his engagement book at home that day, so he said

*Watashi-ga kaettara sugu denwa-shimasu.*
(I'll call you as soon as I get home.)

He thought that this was a perfect sentence, but Mr. Takada still gave him the look that he always had when Mr. Lerner's Japanese was a little strange.

\*　　　　　\*　　　　　\*

In this situation a Japanese would say

*Kaettara sugu denwa-shimasu.*

*Watashi-ga kaettara sugu denwa-shimasu* would mean either that "I" will call rather than anyone else or that someone will call only after I return. In Mr. Lerner's case, there is no need to say *watashi*; including it sounds either strange or misleading.

Another example: when serving tea, a Japanese would not say *Doozo ocha-o nonde-kudasai*. Just *Doozo* or *Ocha-o doozo* is sufficient. *Doozo ocha-o nonde-kudasai* is used in other situation; the meaning will change

# 帰ったらすぐ電話します

*I'll call you as soon as I get home*

　Mr. Takada が Mr. Lerner に、友人を紹介したいから一緒に夕食をしてほしいが、来週いつかあいていないかとたずねた。あいにく手帳を家においてきてしまったので、

　　　　ワタシガ帰ッタラスグ電話シマス

と言った。

　Mr. Lerner としては、これで文は正しいと思ったが、Mr. Takada を見ると、また日本語がちょっと変だったなという顔をしていた……。

　　　　　　＊　　　　　　＊　　　　　　＊

　こういう場面であったら、

　　　　帰ったらすぐ電話します

というのが普通である。

　「わたしが帰ったら電話します」と言うと、「他の人でなくわたしが電話する」、あるいは「わたしが帰ったらだれかが電話する」という意味になる。上記の Mr. Lerner の場合、「わたし」を入れる必要はない。入れると変に聞こえたり、誤解を招いたりする。

　別の例をあげるなら、お茶を出す時、普通は「どうぞお茶を飲んでください」とは言わない。「どうぞ」か「お茶をどうぞ」で十分である。「どうぞお茶を飲ん

depending on what word is emphasized.

> *Doozo OCHA-O nonde-kudasai.*
> (Please have tea rather than something else.)
> *Doozo ocha-o NONDE-KUDASAI.*
> (Please drink the tea rather than doing something else with it—
> throwing it away, for instance.)

Thus, when serving tea, it is correct to say *Doozo* or *Ocha-o doozo.*

Speakers of English tend to think that they should use a complete sentence—complete in the sense of the English equivalent—and try to say *Watashi-ga kaettara denwa-shimasu* or *Doozo ocha-o nonde-kudasai.* If they do this all the time, they give the impression either of sticking to classroom Japanese or being overly specific, boastful, or even aggressive. In order to properly communicate in Japanese, it is important to keep in mind that what seem to be grammatically complete sentences are not necessarily the best.

(August 28, 1977)

でください」を使うのは別の場合で、その場合もどの語を強調するかによって意味が違ってくる。

　　　どうぞお茶を飲んでください

は、「他の物でなくお茶を飲んでください」の意味であり、

　　　どうぞお茶を飲んでください

は、「お茶について、他のこと、たとえば投げ出したりなどせず、飲むという処理をしてください」の意味となる。

　英語を話す人たちは、つい完全文でなければいけないと考えやすい。完全文というのを英語の complete sentence と同じものと考えるため、「わたしが帰ったら電話します」とか「どうぞお茶を飲んでください」と言おうとする。こういう話しかたを続けていると、教室日本語にとらわれている、あるいは自己主張が強すぎるという印象を与える。日本語で適切なコミュニケーションを行うためには、文法的に完全文と思われるものが必ずしも最善ではないことを、銘記することが大切である。

（1977.8.28）

# *Kikoo-no see-deshoo*
## 気候の せいでしょう
### It must be due to the weather

Mr. Okada always complains about his health before starting business discussions with Mr. Lerner and Mr. Takada. Mr. Lerner is often surprised at the patience Mr. Takada shows when listening to Mr. Okada's complaints. He wouldn't be able to stand so much complaining; he would ask Mr. Okada to go home and stay in bed instead of coming to discuss business. Just yesterday afternoon when Mr. Okada complained about his arthritis as usual, Mr. Takada said quietly,

*Kikoo-no see-deshoo.*
(It must be due to the weather.)

and this seemed to satisfy Mr. Okada. Mr. Lerner decided to say this when he was tempted to say "Go home and stay in bed!"

Mr. Lerner was also interested in the phrase . . . *no see*. He was once told by Sensee to be careful in using it because it has the nuance of a reprimand, so he has not used it yet.

        \*        \*        \*

*See* is used to imply that the speaker is unhappy about the situation or angry with the cause, as in

*Ano-hito-no see-de paatii-ga dame-ni natta.*
(lit., Due to him the party became no good.)

# 気候のせいでしょう

### It must be due to the weather

　Mr. Okada は、Mr. Lerner や Mr. Takada と仕事の話を始める前に、必ず体の調子についての愚痴をこぼす。そうした愚痴を聞く時の Mr. Takada の辛抱づよさに、Mr. Lerner はつくづく感心する。自分だったら、あんなにこぼされてはかなわないと思う。それじゃ商談なんかに出向いてくるのをやめて、家へ帰って安静にしてたらどうですかと言ってやるところだ。昨日も昨日とて、いつものように神経痛が痛む話が出ると、Mr. Takada は静かに、

　　　気候のせいでしょう

と言った。それで Mr. Okada は気がすんだようであった。「帰って寝てなさい!」と言いたくなったら、この文句を使うことにしようと Mr. Lerner は決心した。

　「〜のせい」という表現もおもしろいと思った。以前先生に、この言葉は非難のひびきがあるから気をつけるようにと言われたので、まだ使ったことがなかったのだ……。

　　　　　＊　　　　　　＊　　　　　　＊

　「せい」は、話し手が状況に不満をもったり、原因に腹を立てたりしていることを暗に示す。

　　　あの人のせいでパーティーがだめになった

which means "he spoiled the party." Therefore one has to be careful when using *see* with someone's name; the causes which are used very often in everyday conversation are as follows:

*sake-no see*
(due to alcoholic beverages),
*toshi-no see*
(due to age),
*byooki-no see*
(due to sickness), etc.

Nature is so generous that we can place blame on her easily.

*Atsusa-no see-de shigoto-ga hakadorimasen.*
(Due to the heat, we aren't making much progress on the work.)

When one is happy about the situation, *okage* is used to indicate the reason as in

*Ano-hito-no okage-de umaku itta.*
(Thanks to him, it went well.)
*Renshuu-shita okage-de yoku dekita.*
(Because I practiced hard, I could do it well.)

Our students often use *tame* to indicate the cause as in

*Atsusa-no tame-ni shigoto-ga hakadorimasen.*

This is correct but not quite conversational. *Tame* is used mostly to mean "for the sake of" or "for the benefit of" rather than "due to." To show the cause, either *see* or *okage* is preferred in conversation because it reflects the speaker's emotions.

(July 1, 1979)

つまり、「あの人がパーティーをだめにした」のである。したがって、「せい」を
だれかの名前につけて用いる時には、慎重にしなければならない。腹立たしい原
因として日常よく使われるのは、

　　　酒のせい
　　　年のせい
　　　病気のせい

などである。自然も至って寛容で、人間が責めを負わせやすい。

　　　暑さのせいで仕事がはかどりません

というように。
　喜ばしい状況については、その原因を示すのに「おかげ」を用いる。

　　　あの人のおかげでうまくいった
　　　練習したおかげでよくできた

などである。
　原因を示すのに、外国人学習者はよく、

　　　暑サノタメニ仕事ガハカドリマセン

と言う。これも間違いではないが、あまり会話的ではない。「ため」はだいたい
において、「～が原因で」よりは、「～の利益になるように」の意味で使われる。
原因を示すには、話し手の感情を反映する「せい」や「おかげ」のほうが会話的
である。

（1979.7.1）

# *Yasumu wake-niwa ikanai*
## やすむ わけには いかない
### I can't very well take the day off

Mr. Takada had caught a bad cold and seemed very tired, so Mr. Lerner suggested that he leave the office early. Mr. Takada thanked him and said

*Demo, soo yuu wake-nimo ikimasen-yo.*
(But I can't very well do that.)

When Mr. Lerner asked him why he couldn't, he said that he couldn't very well go home early when the others were working hard. Mr. Lerner thought it was no use for a sick person to stay and just make his sickness worse, but he felt interested in the expression . . . *wake-niwa ikanai*. Sensee had once explained to him that . . . *wake-niwa ikanai* or . . . *wake-nimo ikanai* means that one cannot do something because of social reasons. Now that he had heard Mr. Takada use it Mr. Lerner understood what Sensee had meant.

\* \* \*

Of the several expressions used to state inability, . . . *koto-ga dekinai* and *(yasum)enai* are used in any case when one cannot do something; the reason may be physical, social or emotional, while . . . *wake-niwa ikanai* is used when one cannot do something because of social reasons. A business-man will say to his wife who asks him to stay home when he has caught a cold,

# 休むわけにはいかない

## I can't very well take the day off

Mr. Takada がひどいかぜで体力を消耗しているのを見て、Mr. Lerner は会社を早退したらとすすめた。Mr. Takada はありがとうと言ってから、

　　　でも、そういうわけにもいきませんよ

とつけ加えた。

Mr. Lerner が理由をたずねると、他の人が営々と働いているのに、自分だけ早く帰ることはできない、という答えだった。Mr. Lerner は、病人が職場にうろうろしていても、病気を悪くするだけで何にもならないと思ったが、「〜わけにはいかない」という表現には興味を引かれた。以前、先生から、「〜わけにはいかない」あるいは「〜わけにもいかない」というのは、社会的な理由があって不可能だという意味だという説明を聞いたが、今 Mr. Takada が使ったのを聞いて、よくわかった気がした……。

＊　　　　　＊　　　　　＊

不可能を表す表現にはいくつかあるが、「〜ことができない」と "...enai"（休めない）の形は、不可能の理由が何であっても使える。物理的な理由でも感情的な理由でもよい。それに対して「〜わけにはいかない」は、何か対人的な理由があってできない時に用いる。サラリーマンがかぜをひいて、妻に会社を休んでくれと言われた時、

*Yasumu wake-niwa ikanai.*

(I can't very well take the day off.)

because he feels he shouldn't be absent, although his absence may not really inconvenience his colleagues.

When a husband says his wife does not have to buy a new dress, she may say

*Demo, konna furui-no kite-iku wake-niwa ikanai-wa.*

(I can't very well wear this old thing.)

Although it is physically quite possible to wear it, her feelings make it impossible to do so.

Since . . . *wake-niwa ikanai* is not usually used when something is physically impossible, it will be funny to a Japanese to hear something like

*Mada akanboo-da-kara aruku wake-niwa ikanai.*

to mean "Since she is still a little baby, she cannot walk." In this case,

*. . . arukenai.*

is appropriate.

(December 11, 1977)

　　　休むわけにはいかない

と答えるのは、休んではならないと感じるからである。休んで実際に同僚に迷惑
をかけるかどうかは別として。

　妻が新しいドレスを買いたいというのに対して、夫が、そんな必要はないと言
ったとする。妻は、

　　　でも、こんな古いの着て行くわけにはいかないわ

と言うかもしれない。物理的にはもちろん着られるのだが、彼女の感情としては
着られないのである。

　「〜わけにはいかない」は物理的に不可能な場合には使わないのが普通である
から、

　　　マダ赤ン坊ダカラ、歩クワケニハイカナイ

のような文はおかしいと感じられる。この場合は、

　　　……歩けない

のほうが適切である。

（1977.12.11）

# *Moo sorosoro dekakenai-to . . .*
## もう そろそろ でかけないと…
### *If we don't leave soon . . .*

Mr. Lerner invited the Takadas out to a movie last Saturday. When he reached their home, Mr. Takada was busy taking care of his plants in the garden. Mrs. Takada, all dressed up, went down to him and told him that it was time to go. But Mr. Takada was absorbed in his work. Then Mrs. Takada said

> *Moo sorosoro dekakenai-to . . .*
> (lit., If we don't slowly go out now . . .)

So Mr. Takada got ready and the three of them went out together.

When the movie was over Mr. Takada suggested having tea together, but Mrs. Takada said

> *Demo, amari osoku naru-to . . .*
> (lit., But if it gets too late . . .)

After parting from the Takadas Mr. Lerner recalled Mrs. Takada's two sentences and noticed that they were not complete ones. And he realized that he had heard many such incomplete sentences spoken by Japanese.

    \*        \*        \*

Sensee said that Mrs. Takada's sentences were complete sentences in the sense that they conveyed their meanings perfectly well without adding any

# もうそろそろ出かけないと…

*If we don't leave soon . . .*

　先週の土曜日、Mr. Lerner は Takada 夫妻を映画に誘った。Takada 家へ行ってみると、Mr. Takada は庭でせっせと植木の手入れをしていた。すっかり身支度をすませた Mrs. Takada が庭へおりて行って、もう時間だと告げたが、Mr. Takada は手入れに夢中になっている。Mrs. Takada が、

　　もうそろそろ出かけないと……

と言ったので、Mr. Takada も支度を始め、3 人連れ立って出かけた。
　映画が終わると、Mr. Takada はお茶を飲もうと言ったが、Mrs. Takada は、

　　でも、あまりおそくなると……

と言った。
　2 人と別れてから思い出してみると、Mrs. Takada の文は 2 つとも完全な文ではなかった。しかも、こうした不完全文が日本人の話には多い、ということに Mr. Lerner は気がついた……。

　　　　　　　*　　　　　　*　　　　　　*

　先生の言うには、Mrs. Takada の文は、他の語句をつけ加えなくても完全に意を伝えているという意味で、不完全文ではないということだった。最初の文は「もう出かけましょう」、2 番めの文は「おそくなってはいけない」の意味であった。どちらの文も、その意味に関するかぎり、その結果を示す語句をあとに加え

other phrases. The first sentence meant "We should go now" and the second one "We shouldn't stay too late." Each of them can be followed, as far as the stated meaning is concerned, by a phrase indicating what will result, but the addition will change the implied meaning. If she had said

*Moo sorosoro dekakenai-to osoku narimasu.*
(lit., If we don't slowly start now, we'll be late.)

it would have sounded more demanding or as if she were criticizing her husband. A similar thing can be said of the second sentence *Amari osoku naru-to . . .* Probably she meant that if they stayed too late they would take too much of Mr. Lerner's time or cause some other inconvenience. But if she had said that out loud, it might have embarrassed Mr. Lerner. Thus she purposely chose to end her sentences with *. . . to* because of her reserve.

Similarly, *. . . tara* is used when suggesting that others do something. For instance, instead of saying *Moo sorosoro dekakenai-to . . .* you can say *Moo sorosoro dekaketara . . .* (lit., If you slowly go out now . . .) without adding the phrase that usually follows, *doo-desu-ka* (how is it?), meaning "Why don't you go out now?" This is more direct than *dekakenai-to . . .* This is so because *doo-desu-ka* or a similar phrase is always implied after *. . . tara*, while after *. . . to* various statements can be implied, thus leaving more to the listener to interpret for himself.

You will often hear sentences ending in *. . . to*, *. . . tara*, and the like, especially in reserved speech. Leaving the concluding part unsaid in this way is not a sign of poor speaking, but is rather regarded as positively good because it shows consideration towards others.

(May 21, 1978)

ることはできるが、加えると相手に与える印象が変わってしまう。

　もし、

　　　　もうそろそろ出かけないと、おそくなります

と言ったとしたら、調子が厳しくなり、夫を批判しているように聞こえたであろう。「あまりおそくなると……」についても、同じようなことが言える。おそらく Mrs. Takada の意味したのは、あまりおそくなると Mr. Lerner の時間をとりすぎるとか、迷惑をかけるということであったろう。しかしそれを声に出して言ったら、Mr. Lerner も気づまりに感じたであろう。それを考えて彼女はわざと「～と」で文を止めたのである。

　同じように、「～たら」も提案に用いられる。「もうそろそろ出かけないと……」の代わりに、「もうそろそろ出かけたら……」だけを言い、「どうですか」などの語句を省くのである。こちらのほうが「出かけないと……」より直接的である。「～たら」のあとは「どうですか」などの語句と決まっているが、「～と」のあとにはさまざまな内容が含まれる可能性があり、聞き手が解釈を加える余地が大きいからである。

　「～と」「～たら」その他で終わる文は、遠慮がちな話しかたによく使われる。このように結びの部分を声に出して言わないのは、話しかたの拙さを示すものではない。他者への思いやりを示すものとして、積極的に評価されるのである。

（1978.5.21）

# *Nan-to iimasu-ka*

なんと いいますか

*What shall I say?*

A few days ago Mr. Okada was explaining his plan to Mr. Lerner and several others. When he came to a rather complicated part, he paused for a moment and said.

*Nan-to iimasu-ka.*
(lit., What do you call it? or What shall I say?)

Mr. Lerner thought that Mr. Okada was asking his listeners a question, but he didn't know what it was about, so he asked Mr. Okada *Nan-no koto-desu-ka* (What is it about?). But just at that moment Mr. Okada resumed his explanation, completely ignoring Mr. Lerner's question. Later Mr. Takada explained that the *Nan-to iimasu-ka* that Mr. Okada had said was not a question but actually a kind of stopgap phrase similar to the English "er . . ." or "you know . . . ," so nobody had to answer him.

*Nan-to iimasu-ka* is used to indicate that the speaker is looking for the right expression. There are several other words and phrases used for this purpose; *anoo, sonoo, konoo* and *eeto* are used very often. Sometimes the prolonged vowel of the preceding word is used as in *Sore-wa aaa* . . . (Care should be taken not to use English pause sounds such as "er . . ." or "uh . . . ," but only Japanese vowels instead.)

# 何と言いますか

*What shall I say?*

　数日前、Mr. Okada が Mr. Lerner ほか数名の人に、自分の案を説明していた時のことである。やや複雑な部分になると、彼は一瞬話をやめて、

　　　何と言いますか

と言う。 Mr. Lerner は、これは聞き手に対して質問しているのだと思ったが、何の話だかわからなかったので、「何ノコトデスカ」と聞き返した。ところが、ちょうどその瞬間に Mr. Okada は、彼の質問を完全に無視して、自分の説明を再開したのである。

　あとで Mr. Takada が説明してくれたところによれば、Mr. Okada が言った「何と言いますか」は質問ではなくて、英語の "er . . ." や "you know" のような、言葉につまった時のつなぎであるから、だれも返事をしなかったのだそうだ……。

＊　　　　　＊　　　　　＊

　「何と言いますか」は、話し手が適切な表現を探していることを示すものである。同じ目的で使われるものとしては、「あのう」「そのう」「このう」「ええと」などがあげられる。先行する語の母音を引きのばして、「ソレワア」のようにすることもある。（英語の "er . . ." や "uh . . ." のように発音せず、日本語の母音を使うよう注意することが必要である。）

　しかし、「何と言いますか」は上のような語とはやや異なっている。半ば独り言のように自分自身に向かって言うのであるから、質問ではない。実際の意味は

But *nan-to iimasu-ka* is somewhat different from other expressions of this kind. Since it is said half to the speaker himself in a monologue-like way, it is not exactly a question. It actually means "I don't know how I should put this but let me try." When the speaker says this, he is indirectly asking the listener to join him in his search for the right word. It can be taken as a sign of uncertainty, but it can also be taken as consideration towards the listener; many Japanese seem to take the latter view and welcome the appropriate use of this expression as an indication of modesty.

This expression has several variants which are used depending upon the level of politeness; when compared with *nan-to iimasu-ka*, *nan-to mooshi-masu-ka* is more polite and *nan-to iimashooka* sounds softer; *nan-to yuu-ka* is less polite and in very familiar speech *nan-te yuu-kana* is also used.

At any level of politeness, it must be said softly, fading out towards the end, and with a dangling intonation so that it won't be taken as a direct question.

(June 4, 1978)

# *Konna kanji-ni shite-kudasai*
## こんな 感じに してください
### *Please make it like this*

Mr. Lerner went into a barber shop yesterday afternoon. When he sat down, he noticed a picture showing a man with a hair style which he liked, so he pointed to it and told the barber

「どう言うべきかわからないが、言ってみよう」ということである。話し手がこう言う時は、聞き手に対して、一緒になって適切な語を探してくれるように、暗に頼んでいるのである。不確かさの表明ととれると同時に、聞き手への心くばりともとれる。多くの日本人は後者の解釈をとり、謙虚さの表明としてこの表現を正しく使うことを歓迎する。

この表現は丁寧さの度合いに応じて、いくつかの形をもっている。「何と言いますか」に比べて、「何と申しますか」のほうが丁寧であり、「何と言いましょうか」のほうがものやわらかに聞こえる。「何と言うか」はあまり丁寧でない話に用いられ、さらにくだけた話では「何て言うかな」などが用いられる。

発言の方法としては、丁寧さの度合いに関係なく、実際の質問と受けとられないよう、やわらかに、末尾に向かって弱め、引きのばすように言うことが必要である。

(1978.6.4)

# こんな感じにしてください

*Please make it like this*

昨日の午後 Mr. Lerner は理髪店へ行った。腰をおろす時男性モデルの写真が目につき、そのヘアスタイルが気に入ったので、それを指さしながら理容師に、

　　コノ形ニシテクダサイ

*Kono katachi-ni shite-kudasai.*

(Please cut my hair in this shape.)

The barber understood and started cutting his hair. Then a young man came in and sat next to him. He also pointed to the picture and said

*Konna kanji-ni onegai-shimasu.*

(Please do it like this.)

Mr. Lerner knew the word *kanji*, but did not know that it could be used in this way.

*   \*    \*    \**

The word *kanji* by itself means "feeling" or "impression." *Kanji-no ii hito* means "a pleasant person" or "an agreeable person" (lit., a person who gives a good impression). *Donna kanji-no hito* means "what type of person?" A barber or a hairdresser will often ask the customer

*Donna kanji-ga yoroshii-desu-ka.*

(lit., What kind of impression will be good?)

meaning "What style would you like?" And if the customer wants the barber or hairdresser to follow a certain model, he says

*Konna kanji-ni shite-kudasai* or ... *onegai-shimasu.*

Incidentally, *koo-yuu* is also used to mean "this kind of." *Koo-yuu, soo-yuu, aa-yuu*, and *doo-yuu* sound a little more formal than *konna, sonna, anna* and *donna*.

It is grammatically correct to say *Kono katachi-ni shite-kudasai* as Mr. Lerner said. Or some people say while showing an instruction

*Kono toori-ni shite-kudasai.*

(Please do it just as this says.)

と言った。理容師は了承して彼の髪を切り始めた。そこへ若い男性が入ってきて、隣に腰をおろした。その人は同じ写真を見て、

　　　こんな感じにお願いします

と言った。

　Mr. Lerner は「感じ」という語は知っていたが、こんな風に使うことがあるということは知らなかった……。

*　　　　　*　　　　　*

　「感じ」という語そのものは、「感情」あるいは「印象」を意味する。「感じのいい人」は、文字通りには「よい印象を与える人」で、「気持ちのいい人」「好感のもてる人」の意味である。「どんな感じの人？」というのは、「どんな人？」の意味である。理容師や美容師は客に向かってよく、

　　　どんな感じがよろしいですか

とたずねる。「どんなスタイルが希望か」の意味である。客のほうでは、一定のモデルがあれば、

　　　こんな感じにしてください／お願いします

と言う。

　余談であるが、「こんな」の代わりに「こういう」も用いられる。「こういう」「そういう」「ああいう」「どういう」のほうが、「こんな」「そんな」「あんな」「どんな」よりやや改まったひびきをもつ。

　Mr. Lerner が言った「コノ形ニシテクダサイ」も、文法的には間違いではない。事実、仕事の方法を指示した書類を見せながら、

　　　この通りにしてください

These sentences are correct but sound as if you want the listener to try very hard to be exact, and therefore they sound demanding or imposing. It is regarded as considerate to show reserve about your request by using such expressions as

*konna kanji* (this kind of impression),
*konna fuu* (this kind of fashion), or
*konna guai* (this kind of manner).

(May 25, 1980)

# *Shinbun-ni yoru-to*
## 新聞に よると
### According to the newspaper

Yesterday morning Mr. Lerner read in the newspaper that two people had died of shock in the earthquake the night before. He wanted to talk about this news to Miss Yoshida, and started saying

*Shinbun-ni yotte . . .*

to mean "According to the newspaper," and wondered if he was right. Then Miss Yoshida said

*"Shinbun-ni yoru-to"-deshoo?*
(You mean "*Shinbun-ni yoru-to*"?)

と言う人もある。こうした文は正しいことは正しいが、正確を期するための努力を相手に対して要求するという印象を与え、そのため、きびしい、いばった口調になる。

　　こんな感じ
　　こんな風
　　こんな具合

などの表現を用いて遠慮を含んだ依頼をするほうが、思いやりのある態度と言える。

(1980.5.25)

# 新聞によると

*According to the newspaper*

　昨日の朝 Mr. Lerner が新聞を開くと、前夜の地震で 2 人の死者が出たという報道が目についた。Miss Yoshida にこの話をしようと思って、

　　新聞ニヨッテ……

と言ってから、これでよかったかなとちょっと不安になって、言いよどんだ。すると Miss Yoshida は、

　　「新聞によると」でしょう？

and smiled. He remembered that he had made the same mistake before, perhaps more than once.

*　　　*　　　*

While . . . *ni yotte* is used to show the means to do something, . . . *ni yoru-to* is used to show the source of information as in

*Shinbun-ni yoru-to yuube-no jishin-wa kanari ookikatta-soo-desu.*

(According to the newspaper, the earthquake last night was quite big.)

or

*Shushoo-no hanashi-ni yoru-to, genzee-wa shinai-soo-desu.*

(According to the prime minister's statement, taxes will not be reduced.)

To show a source of information, however, several other expressions are used rather than . . . *ni-yoru-to*, which sounds formal; the following expressions are used in daily conversation:

*Shinbun-ni kaite-atta-n-desu-ga . . .*

(It was written in the newspaper that . . .)

*Shinbun-de yonda-n-desu-ga . . .*

(I read in the newspaper that . . .)

*Terebi-no nyuusu-de itte-imashita-ga . . .*

(They said on the TV news that . . .)

And when conveying someone's statement, it is more conversational to say

*Yamamoto-san-ga itte-ta-n-desu-ga . . .*

or

*Yamamoto-san-ni kiita-n-desu-ga . . .*

than saying *Yamamoto-san-no hanashi-ni yoru-to . . .*

(December 21, 1980)

と言って、にこっと笑った。そういえば同じ間違いを前にも、おそらく一度ならず、やっていたのである……。

＊　　　　　　＊　　　　　　＊

「〜によって」が何かを行うための手段を示すのに対し、「〜によると」は情報源を示すのに用いられる。たとえば、

> 新聞によると、ゆうべの地震はかなり大きかったそうです
> 首相の話によると、減税はしないそうです

のように使う。

しかしながら、情報の源を示すのには、改まった感じのする「……によると」よりは、いくつかの他の表現を用いることが多い。日常の話し合いでは、

> 新聞に書いてあったんですが……
> 新聞で読んだんですが……
> テレビのニュースで言っていましたが……

のような表現が用いられる。

また、人から聞いた話を伝える時は、「山本さんの話によると……」より、

> 山本さんが言ってたんですが……

とか、

> 山本さんに聞いたんですが……

のような言いかたのほうが会話的である。

（1980.12.21）

# *Osokatta-desu-ne*
## おそかったですね
### *You're late*

Mr. Lerner and several of his colleagues went on a picnic last Saturday. They met in front of a railway station in the morning, but Mr. Takada was late. When he finally showed up, Miss Yoshida said a little angrily

*Osokatta-desu-ne.*

(lit., You were late, weren't you?)

and Mr. Takada apologized. Mr. Lerner wondered why Miss Yoshida had used the past tense of *osoi*.

\*　　　　　\*　　　　　\*

Both *osoi* and *osokatta* can be used to mean "You're late," but the speaker's attitude is different in the two cases. When one says *Osoi-desu-ne*, one is emphasizing the present state of the person being late, but when one says *Osokatta-desu-ne*, one is emphasizing the fact that a long time had elapsed before he came. In other words, the speaker is more concerned about what has preceded the present state of things than he is about the present state when he uses adjectives ending with . . . *ta*.

Sometimes both forms, the dictionary form and the . . . *ta* form, are used in similar situations. For instance, when thanking someone one sometimes says *Arigatoo-gozaimasu* and sometimes *Arigatoo-gozaimashita*. The latter is used when the speaker wants to emphasize that it has taken a considerable length of time or amount of trouble to complete the action.

# おそかったですね

*You're late*

　先週の土曜日 Mr. Lerner は同僚数人とピクニックに出かけた。朝、駅の前に集合したのだが、Mr. Takada はなかなか来なかった。やっと姿を現したのを見て Miss Yoshida はやや怒った声で、

　　おそかったですね

と言い、Mr. Takada はわびた。しかし、Miss Yoshida はなぜ「おそい」と言わず、「おそかった」と過去形にしたのだろうと、Mr. Lerner はふしぎに思った……。

＊　　　　　＊　　　　　＊

　"You're late." に当たる日本語として、「おそい」も「おそかった」も用いられるが、話し手の態度には違いがある。「おそいですね」と言う時は、おくれて来た人の現在の状況を強調しているが、「おそかったですね」と言う時は、その人が来るまでに長い時間が経過したことを強調している。言いかえれば、形容詞の「た」形を用いる時の話し手は、現在の状況よりもその前に何があったかに関心を持っているのである。

　時には同じような状況で、現在形も「た」形も用いられることがある。たとえば感謝の意を表す時、「ありがとうございます」と言う場合もあるし、「ありがとうございました」と言う場合もある。後者は、その行為が完了するまでにかなり長い時間がかかったか、大変な苦労があったことを、強調したいと思う場合に用いられる。したがって、「ありがとうございました」は言いかえれば、「これまでに多くのことをしていただいてありがたく思います」(Thank you for having done

Thus *Arigatoo-gozaimashita* can be translated as "Thank you for having done so much for me."

Adjectives ending with . . . *ta* can also imply the speaker's psychological involvement in the process by which a certain state comes to an end. For instance, when hearing good news, saying *Yokatta-desu-ne* usually implies that the speaker has been concerned with the matter and is now released from that worry. Thus when you want to express your joy at hearing good news such as someone's having passed an important examination, it is more appropriate to say

*Yokatta-desu-ne.*

than to say

*Ii-desu-ne.*

(October 17, 1982)

# *Gurai, hodo, bakari*
ぐらい、ほど、ばかり
*About, approximately, nearly*

At a little grocery store in the neighborhood Mr. Ernest Lerner was taking some time deciding what fruit to buy, when a woman came in and asked for some pears. When the shopkeeper asked how many she wanted, she said, so much for me.）となる。

　形容詞の「た」の形は、また、ある状況が終結するまでの経過に深い関心があることを示す。たとえば、よい知らせを聞いた時、「よかったですね」と言うと、その事柄にこれまで関心を持ちつづけ、いま心労から解放されたという意味を表す。したがって、だれかが重要な試験に合格としたというような吉報に接して、喜びを表現する時には、

　　　いいですね

と言うより、

　　　よかったですね

と言うほうが適切である。

（1982.10.17）

# ぐらい、ほど、ばかり

### About, approximately, nearly

　Mr. Lerner が近所の小さな八百屋で、くだものは何にしようかと迷っていると、ひとりの女性が入ってきて、ナシを下さいと言った。店のあるじがいくつ包もうかとたずねると、

*Soo-ne, mittsu-gurai.*
(Well, about three of them.)

The shopkeeper picked up three pears and gave them to her. Then another woman came in and asked for apples, saying *yottsu-hodo* (about four).

Mr. Lerner was reminded of what he had observed at the office a few days before. Mr. Takada asked Miss Saito to lend him *sen-yen-bakari* (about ¥1,000). Mr. Lerner wondered if Miss Saito would give him ¥999 or ¥1,001 since she was asked for about ¥1,000. But she merely handed him one ¥1,000 bill, completely ignoring the word *bakari*.

English-speaking people also use such expressions as "about twenty," "a few," or "several," but it seems to many Westerners that Japanese actually dislike giving exact numbers.

*       *       *

The use of such expressions as *gurai, hodo,* and *bakari* shows that the speaker does not want to press the listener by demanding an exact amount. Rather he wants to make the listener comfortable by leaving him some margin for choice. Suppose your friend happened to have only ¥999 to spare when you asked for ¥1,000; he would be embarrassed since he does not want to refuse your request. Although this is a hypothetical example, the underlying idea is such consideration toward others.

Recently this usage, like other aspects of Japanese, is undergoing some change. Young people tend to discard it, feeling that it is meaningless to try to make one's requests vague—if the listener finds your request inconvenient, he can just say so.

However, you will notice in your life here that most Japanese still use *gurai, hodo,* and *bakari* very often, perhaps more often than they realize.

(September 12, 1976)

　　そうね、3つぐらい

と答えた。主人はナシを3つ取って渡した。そこへもうひとりの女性が入ってき
て「4つほど」りんごを買った。

　そういえば数日前にも、会社で同じようなことがあった。Mr. Tanaka が Miss
Saito に「千円ばかり」貸してほしいと頼んだのである。千円ぐらいと言われた
のだから、999 円か 1,001 円でも渡すのかなと思って、Miss Saito を見守ってい
ると、千円札 1 枚渡しただけで、「ばかり」は完全に無視されてしまった。

　英語を話す人たちも "about twenty" "a few," "several" などという表現を使うこ
とは使う。しかし日本人の「ぐらい」「ばかり」の愛用ぶりは、まるで正確な数
字を毛ぎらいしているのかと思われるほどだ……。

＊　　　　　　＊　　　　　　＊

　「ぐらい」「ほど」「ばかり」などを用いるのは、明確な数量を要求することに
よって相手を圧迫することを、望まないからである。ある程度の選択の余地を残
すことによって、相手の気持ちを楽にしようとしているのである。仮に、相手が
999 円しか自由にならないのに、1,000 円貸せと言ったとする。いやとは言いた
くない相手は、困った立場に置かれてしまう。これは現実性の薄い仮定ではある
が、「ぐらい」などを用いる習慣の根底には、相手に対するこうした配慮が働い
ている。

　最近、こうした用法にも変化が見られる。要求の数量を不明確にしようとする
のは無意味だ、要求に応じられなければ、否と言えばいいではないかという考え
かたが、若い人たちの間にひろまりつつある。

　しかしまだ多くの日本人が、自分でも気づかずに「ぐらい」「ほど」「ばかり」
を連発しているのが現状である。

(1976.9.12)